SIXTEEN TO FORTY
A Woman's Story

BY

"MARNA"

NEW YORK
D. APPLETON AND COMPANY
MCMXXVII

Printing Statement:

Due to the very old age and scarcity of this book,
many of the pages may be hard to read due to the
blurring of the original text, possible missing pages,
missing text and other issues beyond our control.

Because this is such an important and rare work, we
believe it is best to reproduce this book regardless of
its original condition.

Thank you for your understanding.

SIXTEEN TO FORTY

SIXTEEN TO FORTY

CHAPTER I

 REMEMBER that I was wearing a silk "duster" with big sleeves, and a flat straw hat that had a great deal of brim in the front and almost none in the back. Under the silk duster I had on a white muslin dress with a foam of little lace-edged ruffles about the hem. I stood, undecided and very young, at the side of the buggy.

"I don't think I ought to come."

"Why not? Oh, why not, Marna? What does it matter? We'll only be out for half an hour or so. You'll probably be back before your mother is. Come on, Marna. Look at the moon coming up. Marna!"

"Oh, all right. I suppose I might as well."

I got in beside him, and even my light weight made the buggy spring and rock. He touched the old horse with his whip and we were off with a pleasing clop, clop, clop, through the darkening streets. The cool air was heavy with flower scents from the gardens along the road. We passed cottages where we could hear the clatter of washing-up after supper, and the

1

voices of mothers calling their children in, and dogs barking, and gates creaking. We went rapidly through the town, and when the horse slowed down he was flicked up again.

"Wait till we get out into the country," Rudy said. "Then you can walk, my friend."

"Where are we going?"

"Oh, just along by the river."

"We mustn't stay out too long."

"I'll take care of you. Don't you worry."

I didn't want him to know how I had longed to come, or how excited I was. I was not seventeen yet, and Rudy was the first young man who had looked away from me with meaning. He did not look at me even now. He was afraid to look, and I knew it. This was my first adventure in love, and I sat upright with childish primness, hardly knowing what to say, and trying to imagine that I was wrapped in furs driving through the snow in a sleigh like Anna Karenina, which I had lately and surreptitiously read.

"Why don't you sit back and make yourself comfortable?" Rudy asked, and I answered:

"I was looking for the moon. I don't know where it's gone to. I saw it just a minute ago." But I relaxed and the dream of Russia fled. This was better, anyway: the cool dusk, and the sweet, reviving air pungent now with the smell of pines and tar-weed,

2

and Rudy sitting beside me, showing only his profile which looked to me sombre and manly, and the old horse with his thin tail swishing about his gaunt hind quarters, and the secrecy of it all and the way we were shut in together there in the buggy's hood.

"Now you can see the moon," Rudy said, and as he spoke it wheeled out from behind some black pine trees on a knoll, and its white stare was almost frightening.

"Isn't it lovely!" I cried, and I heard him sigh; and then he asked the question that youth eternally asks:

"Why do beautiful things hurt so?"

He was still at college and he had come home for his vacation. I had met him perhaps seven times in all, and each time we had been more conscious of one another. I was glad that he had singled me out, glad and flattered, for I was hardly known at all in Cortland, being a newcomer, and poor. My father's inventions had come to nothing, all his hopes were temporarily dashed, and we were spending the summer in a boarding-house in that pretty Northwestern town to save money. The girls I met were inclined to snub me, and although I liked reading books better than talking to girls, it hurt me.

We had reached the bank of the wide river now, and the road, one day to be called a boulevard, ran beside it for miles. There was a dark wall of pines

3

on one side of us, and on the other the liquid shadows and glimmer of the flowing water from which a faint mist rose up to mingle with the moonlight. I was happy and silent.

"Are you cold, Marna?"

"No, not a bit, thank you. I was thinking about what you said."

"About beautiful things hurting? They do. Even your little face hurts me, somehow."

"Rudy, I'm not beautiful. I'll never be beautiful."

"I don't know. You are to me, anyway. You'll be a world-beater by the time you're twenty-five."

My heart raced. Would I? Would I? Was it possible that he was right? I felt my destiny coiled like a snake within me when he said that. And he was a man, not a boy like the other boys I had known.

"Do you think so, Rudy? I wonder! What are you going to be, Rudy? When you get out of college, I mean."

"What would you like me to be?"

"Me? Oh, I don't know. A poet, maybe."

"I'd like to be a poet all right. I believe I could be. But I suppose I'll have to go into my father's tannery. That's life."

"If I were a man," I said, never having thought about it till that moment, "I'd be an engineer and build bridges."

"Would you? Why?"

4

"Oh, I don't know. There's something sort of big about it. And the places you'd go to. . . ."

"Have you ever seen Brooklyn Bridge?"

"Oh, yes, lots of times. I've lived in New York, you know."

"You've travelled a lot for a kid."

"You see, I was born in Paris."

"I know. That's what makes you different, I guess."

"Am I different?"

"Marna, you know you are. I sort of felt you were the first time I saw you. You seemed to be different from the others. You sort of stood out, alone, as though you were lonely, and wanted to be. I don't know how to explain what I felt about you. Gosh! Look at that moon!"

It was quite free of the earth now, hanging—menacing us with its white stare—over the river on which its light poured down. It poured into the buggy's hood and fell full upon my face, and I knew that it made my eyes and teeth shine whitely, and I hoped it made my face mysterious and pale.

"How lovely you look!"

"Oh, do I, Rudy? It's the moonlight."

The old horse was walking now with drooping head. The reins drooped upon his back, the buggy creaked peacefully, and the pleasant smell of old leather mingled with the scent of pines and tar-weed.

"Marna, talk to me. Tell me things. Have you ever been in love?"

"No, not yet. No, never really. I've thought an awful lot about it, though. When I go for walks by myself I think about it, and when I'm sewing and before I go to sleep. And other times, too. It must be wonderful to be in love."

"It is. It's wonderful. But it's agony, too. Marna, you know that little snap-shot you gave me?"

"Yes."

"I've got it in my watch. I'll show it to you."

Our heads drew together as he opened a gold watch that I knew had belonged to his grandfather.

"Can you see?"

"Yes, I can see. Think of looking at a snap-shot by moonlight!"

"It'll stay there," he said, "as long as the old watch lasts, and I guess that'll be all my life. That's how I feel about you, Marna."

"I didn't suppose you'd keep it for a minute," I said.

"Well, I'm going to, always."

"Once," I said, harking back, "I thought I was in love with a choir boy in a church in New York. I never spoke to him, but he had the loveliest face, and I could hear his voice above all the others."

"I suppose he sang for you instead of thinking about God," said Rudy jealously and bitterly.

6

"I don't think so. I don't think he even saw me. I don't know. Sometimes I used to think I caught his eye looking at me. He had black, black hair, and a pale face."

"Funny how girls fall for black hair."

"I don't as a rule. I like brown hair best."

"Honestly?"

"I always mean what I say, Rudy."

"Yes, I know. That's another way you're different from most girls. Marna, take off your hat, it makes shadows on your face and I want to look at your face with the moon on it."

I drew out two long pins, laid the hat on my knee, and stuck the pins into it again. He looked full at me, and I saw in his face what I had never seen in a man's face before, and my pulse went faster.

"You've got your hair up."

"Yes, I put it up to-night."

"For the first time?"

"Yes."

"I believe you did it for me. Please don't say you didn't. What a great pile of it you've got. When it's all down, how far does it come? I've only seen it sort of looped up with a bow."

I blushed, I could feel myself blushing, as I answered.

"Well, it comes a long way below my waist."

"How lovely it must be!"

7

"Rudy, we ought to be turning back."

"Oh, no, good gracious, we haven't been out more than twenty minutes. It's early."

"Yes, but mother——"

"She won't be back for an hour yet. She isn't very strict, is she?"

"Well, yes, in some ways. She won't let me go to dances yet, or go out with boys alone, or read novels."

"What does she let you read?"

"Dickens and Thackeray and Scott, and sometimes Mrs. Humphry Ward. I love Mrs. Humphry Ward."

"But they're novels, aren't they?"

"Yes, but I mean she won't let me read really exciting ones. She won't let me read Ouida, or books like *Red Pottage* or *Unleavened Bread.* But she did let me read *The Cloister and the Hearth,* and there were a lot of things in it I wasn't sure I understood."

"Have you ever read a book called *Tess of the D'Urbervilles?*"

"No, but I've heard of it. Ought I to read it?"

"No. It's a terrible book. Don't read it. I'd hate to think of your reading things like that. I think your mother's right to be careful. I'd like you to stay just as you are, always. It's awful to think that you'll probably change some day."

"Oh, no, Rudy, I won't change. Why should I change? I promise you I won't."

"People do. It's the saddest thing about life, I think. Are you going to college?"

"No. I don't want to."

"I'm glad. Do you ever think about marrying, Marna?"

"Oh, yes, of course I think about it. But I won't marry till I'm at least eighteen."

"That's nearly two years. Do you know I'm almost nineteen?"

"Yes, I know. Sometimes I wish I were, too."

"No, no. You're just the right age. I always think a woman ought to be younger than a man. Just look at that moon now! It looks as though someone was pulling it up the sky by a string."

"Yes, doesn't it? Rudy, do you believe in God?"

"Of course I do. Don't you?"

"I do now. When I was younger I didn't. You see, when I was a child I thought God was a kind old man with a white beard who kept everyone from harm. When I found he wasn't, everything seemed to just go. I lost faith. Do you know what I mean?"

"Yes, I know," he said very solemnly. "It's awful, isn't it? What do you believe now?"

"I believe God is goodness, a sort of lovely spirit, and when we die what's good of us just goes and joins him. And that's heaven."

9

"Oh, Marna, that means you'll go and I won't."

"Rudy, what nonsense! Of course you'll go. Why, I don't know anybody better and kinder than you."

"Do you think I am? I'm not really good, Marna. I've done awful things in my time. A fellow has such temptations. But I'll be good now for your sake, that is, if you care enough. Do you care, Marna?"

"Of course I care, Rudy. I care very much." I added primly, "We ought to be going back now."

"We'll go as far as that hill," he pointed with his whip, "and then we'll turn around."

The hill stood up stark and black, its sides fringed with pines, and cast a wide dark shadow on the road and on the shivering river that bent round it. The horse walked on with lowered head, and in the buggy behind him there was silence. Sitting in my corner, still and withdrawn, I looked at Rudy's profile, and though I had no fear, no wish to turn back, or to evade whatever new thing I was now to learn, I had to remind myself that it was only Rudy, and that he would take care of me and that, although he suddenly seemed almost a stranger, he had my snapshot in his watch.

I kept silent, instinct told me this was not a moment for speech, and even if I moved some spell might be broken, some unknown culmination spoilt. I hardly breathed. I was the soul of passivity, and in

10

that nearing shadow lay a little mark upon my line of fate. My very spirit was ready to proffer its lips to taste the unknown wine. There had been no moment in all my life when I had felt so alive, so conscious of myself, and yet so quiescent. Expectancy and moonlight, and then suddenly the dark, and in answer to a pull on the reins the old horse fell into a slow walk, and the hill's shadow enveloped us all.

Rudy turned toward me with an inevitable and lovely movement, as though he could endure no longer the infinity of inches that separated us. An arm went behind me, and for the first time I knew the intolerable comfort of that support. He gathered me to his side as easily as he might have gathered my dress without my body in it.

"I mustn't let him kiss me," I was thinking in the very moment of defeat. "What will he think of me if I let him kiss me?"

"Oh, Marna," Rudy murmured. "You're so sweet. You're the only girl in the world. Marna, put your arms around my neck. Please, please put your arms around my neck."

I could not speak. I knew how I would hate the sound of my own words, stupid, necessary, protesting words that I would not say for fear of spoiling something lovely.

The horse stopped, and for the first time we heard

11

the liquid whisper of the river. The buggy's hood was a little secret world and there was nothing in the world but my upturned face, and the incredible wonder of our meeting lips.

I had let a man kiss me. I had been kissed. I had let a man kiss me. Finally, unerringly, inevitably. Nothing so exquisite and so solemn had ever happened to us, and we trembled. Our hands were tightly clasped together and in the dark we searched for one another's eyes.

"Rudy, take me back now," came my faint whisper.

"I will, my darling. I'm going to, I promised. Oh, *Marna*——!"

He took up the reins, and the horse, quick to understand and respond, backed toward the bank, turned, and with the enthusiasm of a gratified and elderly governess began the homeward journey. Rudy drove with one hand, the other arm was about my waist. Ashamed and happy, I leaned against him, and thought of those unforgetable kisses, and my cheeks flamed in the dark. I wanted to drive on like this for ever, just like this.

We came to the town again, where lights burned in warm rooms heated by the day's sun, and we saw couples standing under trees and smelt the heavy scent of white flowers, and heard dogs bark. There were lights in the windows of the boarding-house where I lived, and in front of it the strip of lawn looked white in the moonlight.

"Tell your mother I just had to show you the river with the moon on it. Tell her I *made* you come. I'll come around to-morrow and tell her myself. Oh, Marna, I hope she's in. It'll be awful if she isn't back yet, and we could have stayed out a few minutes more."

"I'm sure she's back. I'm afraid it's late. Good-night, Rudy."

"You can't go like that, without kissing me again. Oh, Marna, how can I let you go? Marna, you'll wait for me, won't you? Promise me, promise me you'll wait for me until I have money enough of my own. Even if it's two years. Promise. You will, won't you?"

"Oh, Rudy—if you want me to—only mother— you see I'm not seventeen yet. I'm not going to marry anybody yet. Dear Rudy, I must go now, I must."

I pinned on my hat.

"I'll see you to-morrow. I'll come around about eleven. Marna, you've promised. Remember, you've promised."

"I'll remember. Good-night, Rudy."

"Kiss me just once more."

I fled up the white path, into the house. He watched me open the door, saw me outlined against

13

the yellow light, and I turned and waved my hands before I shut myself in.

I hurried along the corridor to my mother's room.
She had not come back yet. I was glad. I went to
my own room which overlooked a small garden and
into which the moon, which seemed to have watched
me all the evening, streamed brightly, showing me
where the matches lay. I lit a candle, and taking off
my hat I went to the mirror. I held the light up
and scrutinized my face. Surely it had changed—
lips, eyes, they could not look the same. Surely,
surely I was different?

Rudy had asked me to wait. What did he mean?
Wait? How could I wait? Time went on, I would
go on. My father and mother were taking me to New
York as soon as my father could get some money, and
New York was three thousand miles away. How
could I wait?

I blew out the candle and threw myself, without
undressing, on the bed; and immediately I was within the buggy's hood again, in the shadow of the hill,
and Rudy was turning towards me.

CHAPTER II

 GLANCED over my shoulder guiltily, and saw that he was watching me from the doorway. Our eyes met and mine tried to convey to him: "I had to dance this dance —he made me—you were late. It was not my fault." His look was, in a wry way, humorous and sardonic. I knew that look so well, it was on his face so often. He followed me about with an air of shame and amusement, but also with an air—and this concerned me most—of not being able to help himself. He hated dancing, and I had promised to sit out this one and the next one with him, and while I waited, his young friend Howard had made me dance with him.

"There's old Sanford over there, looking for you," my partner said.

"Yes, I know, I saw him. I thought he must have forgotten after all."

"Forgotten? Not he!"

"Well, let's dance over to him and then I must stop."

"Oh, hang it, must we? He's always butting in. I never get a chance. And I love this tune."

The small, lively Yacht Club band was playing

15

"Bedelia," a brisk two-step. But Howard did as he was told, and when we were beside Sanford, he said:

"It's your own fault, old man, for being slow."

Sanford was smiling, but it was the smile, I could see plainly enough, of a man who tries not to show that he is hurt. I was not very old then or I would also have guessed that the sight of me dancing with his younger friend had aroused a tumult of jealousy and bitterness in him, and that he regretted and hated his own emotion.

"Come along, child," he said, still smiling. "You can dance when I am dead."

His assumption of great age always amused and pleased me. He was only thirty-nine, but he talked as though he were ninety, and it increased my fondness for him. He was a lawyer, and clever, with a cleverness that frightened me and made me diffident, for it was the only thing about him I felt I did not understand. He had a face that was half comic, half tragic, as lawyers, I was later to learn, so often have, and it gave promise in old age of a sort of lovable crabbedness. His small green eyes were deeply shadowed by black, mobile brows. It was an Irish face, and I think his grandparents had come from Ireland. He was slight and not tall, and walked defiantly and purposefully. I was secretly very proud that he spent so much of his time with me and, in a childish way, I loved him.

16

"I was stopped outside," he explained, "for two minutes. You're like life, you're like time, aren't you? You can't wait for anything or anyone. You're perfectly right. There's nothing and no one worth waiting for. All the same, Mrs. Grundy willing, I shall keep you to myself for half an hour or so."

"As long as you like," I said, touched with remorse. "I don't want to dance any more. I'd rather talk to you."

"We'll go and look at the lights in the harbour," he said, and led the way along the sheltered porch that ran the length of the club-house. There, in a far corner, he had put two chairs together, and to keep them had draped my white shawl across them both.

"I suppose that idiotic boy Howard is in love with you?"

"I don't know." I didn't know, and I wondered very much. "He hasn't said so."

He laughed.

"Neither have I said so. You must make what you can out of it, child. Well, well—do you realize I've been waiting about for over an hour, holding your shawl and boring myself while you danced?"

"I don't suppose you'd do it if you didn't want to."

"I wonder? There are different sorts of wanting, as you'll discover one day, if you haven't already. There's a protesting voice within me that raises bit-

17

ter lamentations and calls me a fool. That same voice tells me you'd rather be dancing with young Howard now than talking to me. Would you? Be honest with me."

"No, I wouldn't. I'd rather be here with you."

"Why? He's young and gay, and when he's my age he'll be miles ahead of where I am now. I'm fond of the boy, but how long I shall remain fond of him if he makes love to you, God alone knows."

No man, however successful, can know the thrill of fearful delight and of power a woman feels when she hears words like these.

"Oh, Sanford—I'd be miserable if you—if he—I do like him, but I like you best." Familiar as I already was with the spectacle of men in love, such moments still disconcerted me, still made me feel young and gauche. I was like a savage who holds in his hands a dangerous and complicated weapon he does not understand how to use. "I hope you'll always be my friend, and talk to me. You can teach me such a lot. You will, won't you?"

"What sort of things, for pity's sake, do you want to learn from me?"

"Oh, anything, everything. I feel so ignorant. I am ignorant. I've never been to school, there never was time, we were always travelling about. And what governesses don't and can't teach you is a good deal more than what they do. I'm alone such an awful

lot. Mother likes to sew and read novels and talk
to people of her own age who don't interest me, and,
having no brothers or sisters, it means I'm by myself
most of the time. You can tell me what I ought to
think and read and study. You've helped me a lot
already."

He was silent for a moment.

"You've had a curious life, haven't you? Short
as it is, it's been full of changes and ups and downs."

"Oh, yes. Never knowing from month to month
where we're going to be next, or whether we'll be able
to pay our bills or not. And not daring to go back
to places sometimes, until father can find money
enough to pay what we owe there. It isn't his fault.
If people won't believe in his inventions he can't
make them, I suppose."

"What's he working on now?"

"Oh, it's rather wonderful. He's invented a new
sort of spirit that burns, and he says it will take the
place of gasolene for automobiles. He says oil is
going to give out soon, all over the world, and then,
of course, he'll make a fortune out of this spirit."

"Won't you have any money till then?"

"He gets a little money now from that patent bot-
tle-opener he invented. A percentage, I think. But
it doesn't sell really well. All the things that sell
well have been stolen from him. I don't know how
long we'll be able to go on like this. I want to try

to earn my own living, but he won't hear of it. He says my job is to stay at home with mother and look after her."

"What will you do when you leave here?"

"I suppose we'll have to go back to that awful boarding-house in New York where we were before. I hate it, it's dingy and horrible, and full of the most awful people. There are two foreigners, one fat and one thin, who stare at me, and untidy women with little dogs, and old men nobody wants, who try to get invited out to dinner on Sundays. I don't think I can bear it again. I've never been so happy in my life as I have here. I wish it didn't have to end."

"Poor child. Well, I've been happy, too, in a strange, dangerous sort of way. I come back here every day after the heat and dust of New York, and it seems like a little heaven. I change, dine—as quickly as I can—and then I take my stick and follow the path along the rocks and through the woods to your hotel, and there you are, sitting in some dim corner of the porch, sometimes alone, but more often, you little demon, with Howard or some other young man, and I grit my teeth and outstay them like any callow lad of the village, until your mother comes and calls you in. It's the middle of September now, alas! and in a few days I'll go back to my rooms in Fifty-Fifth Street, and it will mean good-bye to all this——!"

20

"Oh, Sanford! Do you mean I'm not going to see you again till we come to New York in October?"

My hand was on my knee, and suddenly his covered it, and he did not answer. We sat there very quietly and we could hear the yacht bells in the little harbour, and the splash of oars. The band inside the club-house was playing some lively tune—I think it was "The Glow Worm and the Moth," and the light breeze that came in from the Sound was fragrant with salt and the green smell of reeds and marsh grass.

"Did you read those books I sent you?" he asked. He kept his hand on mine, and I knew he did not want to go on speaking of what would happen after he left. The warmth from his hand penetrated mine and I kept it very still for fear a movement might make him take it away. And, although it gave me some comfort, a lump came into my throat.

"Oh, yes, I loved them both. I think I liked *Aftermath* a little the best, but *The Kentucky Cardinal* was lovely, too. Thank you for giving them to me, Sanford. I just love the way they're written."

"Gracious heavens, child! That's three loves in one breath, almost."

"What ought I to say, then? Anyway, it's true, I did love them, and I meant what I said. You're very unkind to-night."

"No, no, I can't be unkind to you. Give me your

21

hand." I had taken it away. He kissed it, and held it more closely in his. "Listen, Marna, you're different from the other young things who infest this place, and places like it. Entirely different. You've got some quality that they haven't. You've got the germ of something unusual in you. I've watched it, I know it's there. I think you're half conscious of it yourself. This won't make you conceited. I don't think anything would. You could no more be conceited about yourself than an ambitious young climbing plant could be. You're straining upwards to get into the sunlight now, and you won't blossom until you get there. How late that blossoming will be depends on circumstances, but I don't think it will be soon. That's why I can't—you're so young—— Oh, if only you were thirty instead of seventeen, how I could talk to you, and if you were thirty, how differently we would talk!"

He suddenly stopped speaking and, putting out his other hand, he turned my face towards him, and in the dim light looked closely into it.

"Marna, the truth is I'm in love with the woman you're going to be, and it's nearly killing me. It's no fault of yours, it's no fault of mine. I never meant to say these things to you, but to-night I can't keep them back. Some women make men love them because of the glamour of their past, but it's your future that I love. I can see it at times like an extension of yourself, all around you. It's the woman you will be who draws me over to that dim porch every night. I wonder if you'll understand this? Do you, child?"

He still looked closely into my face, as though he were looking for that woman who was myself and yet not myself. A tear fell from my eyes and splashed down upon his hand.

"You're crying, and it's I who ought to cry, because I'm too old. I've never seen you cry before, I can't imagine that inquiring little nose reddened with tears, though I should like it just the same. I'm sorry, I'm sorry if I've hurt you."

I tried to control my voice.

"I know what you're trying to tell me. That I'm not going to see you any more."

"I must get to work with an undivided mind. I hardly dare look my books and briefs in the face."

"What you really mean is that you won't compete any longer with Howard, and with those Effingham boys who have been boring me to death. I don't care about any of them. I'll get rid of them all. I'd a million times rather be with you, Sanford. I would, I would. You can teach me things, you're so much older and cleverer than they are——"

"I felt a murderous rage to-night when I saw you dancing with Howard. I felt sick with the most outrageous and illogical pain. I felt that, *I*, who for

23

years have cherished an entirely humorous and sophisticated view of love, and the pleasures and pains
of love!"

I cried out——

"Just because I'm young, just because I'm ignorant,
you hate yourself for being fond of me. You're
ashamed of it. It isn't fair! It's cruel! Who will
help me if you don't?"

Tears were running down my cheeks now, and I
did not want to stop them. I felt miserable—de-
feated. I thought I had power over him, and I found
I had none at all. He was going to leave me and
never see me again, and nothing that I could do or
say would keep him.

He got up and pulled me to my feet. The porch
was deserted. The band had just begun to play a
waltz called "Kiss Me Again," that Fritzi Scheff had
made famous and it had drawn everyone in as honey
draws flies. I leaned on his shoulder, sobbing quietly.

"Marna, dear child, don't cry. If you knew how
sad I was, you'd be sorry for me. If I hadn't lost my
head over you so fantastically, I might be your
friend, but it's no good, I've learnt my lesson, and
as for help you'll help yourself better than I could
help you. If you ever need me, if you're ever in
trouble, write to me, but I'm going to leave the field
after to-night."

I clung to him, crying still, shaking with sobs.

My grief must have frightened him. He held me gently, patiently, waiting for the storm of sorrow to pass. Then suddenly he whispered, putting his lips to my ear:

"Marna, Marna, would you marry me?"

Sanford as a husband—marriage—it had never entered my head. I could say nothing, but it changed my thoughts a little and stemmed my tears. Tenderly he kissed my hair and patted my shoulder, then let me go, and I dried my eyes, for I heard voices. I understood perfectly that my misery had startled him, and that he wanted to make sure he had not mistaken its cause. He was silent, giving me time to recover, and when he heard me give a deep sigh—one of those sighs that are apt to follow tears—he asked, very quietly:

"Who is going to take you home?"

"Howard said he would."

"Sit down again, it isn't late, and we'll talk and I'll tell you what sort of things I'd like you to read."

I sat and listened to him, as I had listened so often before, and every now and then the tears rushed back to my eyes, and as often as they came I wiped them away with a small handkerchief that was already wet. I believed that my life would be empty and desolate without him, though I had known him only seven weeks, and I did not see how I was going to bear it. My life was precarious and hard, with few pleasures.

25

I doubted if I would even be able to buy the books
he was telling me to read. This friendship I had
treasured so, and of which I was so proud, would
soon belong to the past. It seemed to me that existence was unutterably sad and perilous. But I could
not have said "yes" to his question. That was unthinkable. It was as though I were on a moving train,
headed for some definite but unknown destination,
and someone had asked me to step off. I loved him,
but I loved him childishly, and I loved best what he
gave me of his mind. It was that I wanted, and
wanted desperately and hungrily. Was it my fault,
I wondered, that I was losing him? If I had been
less ignorant—I could not help being young—could
I have kept him? If I had waited for him this evening instead of dancing with Howard, would it have
been different? The thought that it might made the
tears rush to my eyes again, and I clenched my hands,
determined to keep them back.

"Are you listening? Don't bother yet with anything but the sketchiest history of Rome. Concentrate on Greece. You can go on to Rome later. I'll
send you a list of the books on Greece, and if you
get puzzled about anything, write to me. And I'll
send you that book on the Renaissance I told you
about, later on. I think Pater will please you more
in a year or two. You asked me once about philosophy. I think you're too young. I don't know what

you believe, but if you want to keep your little religious views intact, you'd better leave Hegel and Kant alone, for ever. What do you believe, Marna? What do girls like you think about life?"

"I think it's vile, horrible," I said.

"Admitted," was his answer. "But what do you think we're here for, and where do you think we're going to, and do you think there's a God? Tell me."

"I think we're here just so that the things we like and the people we're fond of can be taken away from us, and I don't believe we're going anywhere, except into the ground, and I think there's only a God for rich people."

"Marna, Marna, we've so little time left."

"It's not my fault," I said, "that we've so little time left."

He changed the subject.

"I'd like you to read Samuel Butler. I'll send you *The Way of All Flesh*. Write and tell me what you think of it. I don't want you to be a little grind, but don't read silly novels, because you'll have such fun with books if you form good tastes and habits early. And above all, read poetry. Good poetry. Read it and read it and read it."

I caught at a sentence of his.

"I may write to you then, may I?"

He sighed, leaned nearer to me, and slipped an arm behind me.

27

"Lovely child, I oughtn't to kiss you, but I must. Marna, turn your face towards me. I must kiss you once. I must."

But my grievances, my sense of defeat, made me hard and bitter. I was ashamed of having failed, and his touch and words hurt me more than they moved me. I pushed him away.

"No. You hate yourself for liking me. Why should I let you kiss me?"

Afterwards I would have given anything to have had that first—and last—kiss. Afterwards I remembered that he had had tears in his eyes and on his eyelids. I had a short note from him the next day, that I kept for years, among other such letters. He said he had loved me four-dimensionally, for his love had been extended into time, and that he was very sad. He sent me his own copy of *The Way of All Flesh* and the *Oxford Book of English Verse*. I do not think he could have been more miserable than I was. It was little consolation to me to know that I had been a victim of Time, especially when my mother would say, as she often did: "We don't see anything of Sanford any more." Or, "What's become of your lawyer friend, Marna?" For I could not explain to her. The pain had gone too deep. It was the first time I had suffered because of a man.

CHAPTER III

 I WAS between eighteen and nineteen when I discovered that I liked kissing for kissing's sake. I did not make this discovery without a good deal of shame. I admitted it to no one—for there was no one with whom I could have discussed such a dark subject—and I believed that it was an evil trait, and that I was very far from good. Before this time, a kiss was to me something exquisitely solemn and sacred, to be employed, rightly, only for the sealing of romantic compacts. Once these compacts were sealed, it became the beautiful coinage of love between husbands and wives. Although passionate and full of feeling, I was innocent and sentimental, and it is to sentiment even more than to innocence that I attribute my immunity in those early years, from all but the lightest and most transient emotions.

Such ballads as *The Rosary* moved me to facile dreams or tears, and I believed that when love, "real" love, came, I should be caught up into a sort of rosy heaven where I should be transformed into quite a different being, and all life "remoulded nearer to the heart's desire"—for I knew my Omar and carried it about with me bound in limp green suede, its lines heavily underscored by my untutored pencil. If Sanford had only remained my friend and adviser for another eighteen months, what a lot of literary calf-loves I might have avoided! But younger men, like Howard, took his place, filling it only indifferently well, and they taught me little but that I was, for some reason I could not fathom, attractive to them.

I read, when they came my way, the books he had recommended to me, but there was no one with whom I could talk about them, and the unrelated scraps of knowledge I gained in this way drifted about my unfurnished mind like leaves blown in through an open window.

I used to spend more time in front of my mirror than Sanford would have liked, slipping the shoulder-straps of my unlovely underclothes off my shoulders to see what I would look like in evening dress, and pinning flowers in my hair. On these occasions I rouged my cheeks by rubbing them with one of the petals of a red rose that trimmed my hat. I wore, uncritically, the few dresses my mother and I made for me, but we were vague as to styles and cut, and I have no doubt they were curious affairs. We had very little money and were living in a boarding-house in West Eighty-ninth Street, where a young Dane and a middle-aged German photographer paid me a good deal of unwelcome attention. My father was in Chicago, trying to sell a new kind of machine to the meat-packers there, so we were alone, and life was very dull. My mother made temporary friends wherever she went, but I made almost no friends, and tried to make myself believe I did not want them.

One day a cousin of my mother took pity on me and asked me to a fancy dress dance given by a friend of hers in Gramercy Park. It was my first venture into anything like "Society," and full of dread and excitement I said I would go. What could I find to say to strangers? I felt there was nothing to talk to them about but the books I had been reading, and not all men, I had learnt, cared to talk about books or even read them. And what should I wear?

A coloured sewing-woman, as black as the inside of a tunnel, came to take my measurements, and carried home with her a pile of white tarlatan. I loved white, and I had decided on a crinoline dress, to be trimmed with pink roses. I shall never forget the blackness of her hands against the pure white of my dress, nor the bright gold spectacles she wore, nor her round, woolly head. On the afternoon of the dance a hair-dresser came and did my hair in ringlets on each side of my face, and coiled it up in a chignon behind. When I was ready I mourned that I could not always look as I did then. I thought I was like a great white bell that could have been picked up and rung.

31

My mother's cousin, elderly and poor, knew almost no one at the dance, and my hostess I saw only once, so there was no one to find partners for me. Introductions were necessary, as we were not masked—or necessary to everyone but a young man, who looked as though he had stepped off the stage of *La Bohème,* and who had seen me standing by the door with a stiff, miserable little smile on my lips, ready to tell my cousin that I wanted to go home. He made me dance with him—though heaven knew I was willing enough—and he told me he was an artist and that he was just back from Paris—Paris, where they knew how to give fancy dress balls. He seemed to hate New York, to hate his fellow countrymen, to hate everyone at the dance. When I told him I had been born in Paris he was ready to fall at my feet. He held me very tightly as we danced, and told me I had the look of a Renoir.

He had a weak, charming face, blue eyes and smooth, soft hair. He told me almost at once that he was engaged to a rich Boston girl, but that he was not sure he loved her, or that her money would not ruin his career. My spirits fell then. An engaged man was the same as a married man to me until that night, and a married man was the mere half of a whole.

We sat on the stairs and he told me that the modelling of my face and head was beautiful. I did not believe him. I never at any time believed what my admirers told me about my appearance. How could they know me better than I knew myself, and was I not aware of every imperfection, every bone, every hollow? But these comments, though I tore them to pieces afterwards, pleased me at the time.

"Why do you live in New York? Why don't you come back to Paris? Paris is the only city in the world fit to live in."

"I will some day. I can't now. I tell you we're poor, really poor. We can't afford to travel."

"How awful the lack of money is! It's so cramping and limiting. Especially here. That's why I'm marrying for money in about six weeks."

"Oh, how can you say that?" I cried, shocked. It's horrible. You mustn't say it."

"It's true. Anyhow, the whole thing's horrible. Marriage is horrible. Think of the awful vows I shall have to make, vows that I can't possibly keep."

"Does she love you?" I asked.

"Yes. That's how the whole thing happened. She told me she loved me. I wasn't thinking of marrying anybody. I was staying in Boston with some relations in Beacon Street, and we kept meeting. The worst of it is I want money, and I can't earn it by painting till I get to the top. Do you think her money will help me get there, or will it keep me from getting there? That's the question I ask myself all the time."

"You ought to think more about her," I said sagely, "and less about yourself."

"Oh, she's all right. I'll be kind to her, and she's getting what she wants. Answer my question."

"I don't know. I don't know anything about it. Not many painters have been rich, have they? Let's see, there's Rembrandt—he was terribly poor, and——"

"Well, but Velasquez was rich," he interrupted me, "and Botticelli was subsidized by rich men, and Van Dyck never knew poverty. I don't think I've got the sort of temperament that flourishes under adversity. But, on the other hand, I can't paint in Boston; the atmosphere's all wrong, and her parents want us to live in Boston. So do mine. They seem to think it's immoral to live in Paris. I sometimes wonder if I'm not a changeling. Have you ever wondered if you weren't?"

"Yes," I confessed. "I don't feel a bit like either my father or my mother. I don't mean I'm better. I'm not. I mean I'm different."

"Of course you are. You ought to live in Europe. You're not like these girls here. American girls are the best-looking in the world and the least interesting. Why, any little French midinette has more understanding of life than these girls have, with their

34

cotton-wool existences and their silly, conventional ideas. I can't talk to them."

"Can you talk to your fiancée?" I asked.

"No. That's where the rub comes. She can talk to men, but I can't talk to her. When she talks about art she makes my flesh creep. She's full of soul, and I hate soul. Painting is chiefly sweat and brains and a hunger for beauty. You can't make these people see it."

"You seem to think I'm different," I said. "Why do you?"

"Well, you've had a hard time for one thing. The good things of life haven't just dropped into your lap like ripe plums. And you've got temperament. I can tell that by your mouth, and by the width across here." He spanned my eyes with a thumb and finger. "I wonder what'll become of you. I think you look perfect in that white dress. I said you were like a Renoir, but I see now you're much more like a Goya."

"I'm awfully ignorant about painting," I said. "I've heard of Goya, but I've never heard of Renoir. I know a little about painters like Titian and Rembrandt and Velasquez and Gainsborough, and I like Rembrandt the best of all, but perhaps I shouldn't. I do want to learn more, but I don't know how to go about it. I feel as though I were stuck fast in a nightmare, and can't get any further. Now and then I

35

meet someone like you, who makes me want to learn things and be something, but most of the time I just grow like a turnip. I want a different sort of life, but I don't know how to get it. It's awful just being a young girl with no money and no sort of home. I'm sick to death of it."

"Why don't you go to an art school? Perhaps you could paint."

"But that costs something, and I tell you I can't even afford car fare sometimes. Nobody understands what it means to have *no* money. And if I leave my mother alone all day she gets terribly depressed. I promised my father I wouldn't."

"Yes, but if you married—why don't you marry? I'll bet you've had chances already."

"I know. But I can't. I don't know why I can't, but I can't, and that's all there is to it. Something won't let me. I've liked people an awful lot, too, but the moment I think of marrying them I go cold all over, and I know I can't do it."

"You funny kid. Most girls would. But I know what you mean. I go cold all over when I think of marrying Elizabeth, but I've got to do it."

"Well, I wouldn't marry anyone I didn't love for anything. I'd rather die."

"Oh no, you wouldn't. Don't you fool yourself."

"I tell you I would."

"Anyhow, what do you know about love?"

"A lot," I said with bravado.

"Have you ever been in love? I don't believe it."

"No," I confessed, "but I know what it feels like *not* to be in love. And I have been fond of people."

"Fond! What a horrible, girlish word! Now that's a word Frenchwomen don't understand, thank heaven. They love, or they don't love. And when a Frenchwoman loves—but I guess I oughtn't to talk to you like this. You're too young."

"I'll be nineteen in five months," I told him.

"You look even younger. Let's run off to Paris together. We'll live in an attic on onion soup and French bread, and I'll paint you all day long."

I laughed, rather shyly. While I was enjoying myself very much I felt he was perhaps rather dangerous and that I was letting him go too fast. I was full of prim and conventional ideas which existed side by side with a certain recklessness which came from repression. I was just clever enough to hide the primness when I was with people who might make fun of it, for I hated being laughed at.

I suddenly remembered my chaperon.

"We've been sitting here for ages," I said. "You'd better go and dance with somebody and I'll wait here till you come back. I don't know anyone else to dance with."

"Neither do I," he said, "and I don't want to. What does it matter how long we stay here? Who's going to notice? Can't your aunt, or whatever she is, leave you here? I'll take you home."

But it was my first big dance and, even though it might also be my last, I wanted to do the proper thing. I would go home as I had come. He begged and teased, his eager, attractive face close to mine, but I would not be persuaded. When he saw that I meant to have my way, he stopped at once, and said: "You're quite right. I feel too reckless and wild to-night to be any young girl's companion."

And at once I regretted my firmness, for I felt it would have been a delightful adventure to have let him take me home.

But for his presence the dance, from my point of view, would have been a ghastly failure, but as it was I loved it and went home excited and happy. My mother's cousin believed me when I said that I had had plenty of nice partners. Realizing her uselessness, she had been playing bridge most of the time, for I had assured her I could take care of myself, and now I was thankful for it. I dreamt about Frank Bellamy that night. I thought he was showing me hundreds and hundreds of pictures, and telling me who the artists were, and as fast as he spoke their names, I forgot them.

For several weeks New York was transformed for me. It became a city of surprises, full of picture-galleries I had not known existed, and florists that yielded me bouquets, and secluded and delightful tea-places.

I think I must have been temporarily bewitched, for although I knew he was going to Boston in a little while to marry his Elizabeth, and that he had no business to be falling in love with me, I could not forego the joy of his companionship, nor could I, after the first short struggle with myself and with him, forego his kisses. I became deceitful and, in order that my mother would not think I was seeing too much of him, slipped out to meet him under the pretext of going for a walk. After our second meeting I knew well enough what was coming. Every look of his from that time was a caress, and every look of mine must have seemed to him an invitation.

An empty room at the Metropolitan Museum framed our first kiss. When his face approached mine, as the steps of the attendant receded, I pleaded with him in whispers not to touch me, but my face remained turned toward his, and I made no effort to draw myself away from the arm about my shoulders. After that, we could not have kisses enough. It was at the same time innocent and dangerous, foolish and sweet.

"Oh, Marna!" he cried one day. "If you only had a little money! Just a little."

"If only I had!" I answered. But at the bottom of my heart I knew I did not want to marry him, that

I was glad he could not marry me. He was an episode, and I knew it. How I knew it, I could not have told.

"Could you live with me on just a little? Not here. In Paris, or even in London, or Dresden. Could you, supposing we had it?"

"I've always been poor," I said. "I wouldn't mind that. But you're going to marry Elizabeth, and—oh, all this is wrong and foolish!"

"It's the sweetest and best thing that's ever happened to me, my darling, and if only we had a little money between us, I'd run off with you. But it may be years before I begin selling pictures. People seem to think only dead artists are any good. The fools! Oh, Marna, how can I live without you? You're so lovely, and I could teach you anything. You could pose for me half the day and we'd talk and look at pictures the other half. What a heavenly life!"

"You've taught me how to look at pictures, and to love them," I said.

"Haven't I taught you to love me?"

I shook my head. I had never said I loved him, and I never did say so.

He would tell me about his life in Paris as a student, and about the other students, and for the first time I saw something of the inside of a man's mind. He was twenty-six, and although he was mature in some ways he was curiously young in others. We used to walk along Riverside Drive in the mornings, shivering in the cold blasts from the Hudson, and watch the light change on the bare Palisades across the river, and he would talk to me about Monet and Manet and Degas and Daumier. We saw only nurse-maids and children, and couples like ourselves. And I remember one of many winter afternoons, at dusk, when the snow flakes whirled about the street-lamps, and the smooth, black ice of the river whitened under its soft burden, and the wind sang in a thin minor voice in the bare boughs of the trees over our heads. We walked close together, his arm through mine, and my hands buried in a small, worn muff that belonged to my mother. The snow had blue shadows on it where the lamps shone through the branches, and it creaked under our feet.

He was talking about Elizabeth, and I begged him not to marry her.

"It has nothing to do with me," I said, "because we can't marry anyway, and I don't think I'd marry you if I could."

"Then why do you kiss me as you do, if you don't love me?"

"I don't know," I said. "I suppose because I like it, that's all. But, Frank, if you marry her you'll make her unhappy and you say you'll be unhappy yourself. Why don't you go back to Paris and give up the idea of marrying until you can earn money?"

But he was honest about his weaknesses, and he said he could not, that he was too fond of luxuries. He liked everything about that old life in Paris except its discomforts.

"I want a tiled bathroom with nice fittings, I want plenty of clean, well-brushed clothes, and nice linen. I want comfortable, warm rooms. If I could have married you I'd have put up with a certain amount of poverty, but without you, what's the good? I might as well follow the line of least resistance."

"Oh," I cried, "you never seem to think of her, and you'll make her miserable."

"No, I won't. She has an orderly mind and she likes house-keeping, and she wants to look after me, and she'll never ask for love because she doesn't know what it is. I'm the one who knows. I'm the one to be pitied. Yes, I'm the one who knows, Marna darling." He held me and kissed me, and we walked on again. "Marna, in a week I shall have gone. It's horrible to think of. And I love you so."

It was horrible for me to think of by that time, because he filled such a gap in my empty, confined life. I would miss him, I would miss his talk, most of all I would miss his love. I raised my face and he kissed me again, and my cheeks were wet with snow. My life seemed made up of episodes, none of which led anywhere, but all of which left something behind them, as tides leave sea-weed and shells upon a beach.

We said good-bye one afternoon in the warm, bright tea-room of the Manhattan Hotel, while an orchestra played "The Rosary" and the latest waltz, and then—for the room was full of sentimental couples—"The Rosary" again, by request. I felt mournful and tears came into my eyes, but I am afraid they were tears of self-pity. Frank sat leaning forward, his hands between his knees, his face the picture of despair. I have often wondered why I was not in love with him, and I think it was the knowledge of something weak and vacillating and selfish in his character that prevented it. And I do not think I ever believed in his talents. I was very fond of him, and certainly he attracted me, but he inspired no confidence in me. I had acted weakly and foolishly myself, I admitted it, but I hated weakness in men.

"I'm going to see you home," he said later, when it was time to go. We had arranged to say good-bye then and there and I believed it was better like that.

"No, please don't," I protested. "It will only make it harder." He smiled at me, and I gave in and followed him outside where we got into a cab. It was a black and white scene out of doors, and the only colour anywhere was the lamps' yellow light. It had begun to snow again, and the dirty heaps beside the gutters that had not yet been taken away were made clean once more, and the passing vehicles made sharp black tracks in the light half-inch fall that covered the streets.

He took me in his arms and kissed me wildly, and I kissed him wildly in return.

"Oh, Frank," I cried, "I've always known this time would come, but it's awful saying good-bye."

"I can't say it," he whispered. "I can't."

He was suffering more than I had dreamed he would, and I was suddenly shocked and frightened. I told him it would be all right once he was in the train—he was leaving that night—and that he must not give way. He groaned and pressed my hands over his eyes, saying my name over and over. When we reached my door my heart was like lead. I kissed him once more, where his forehead met his fair hair, and ran into the house, and he drove on.

I was very quiet at dinner and my mother asked me if I were not feeling well. After dinner she sat down to a game of bridge with an old lady and a Mr. and Mrs. Something-or-other, and I went up to my room with a book—it was a novel called *Amos Judd* —and sat in an armchair close to the radiator.

Presently someone knocked on the door, and I heard the voice of the coloured porter saying I was wanted on the telephone. I ran downstairs and into the booth at the back of the hall, my heart pounding, for I feared I do not know what.

It was Frank. He said he could not go to Boston, that he was not going, that he would rather shoot himself than go.

"I've got a gun here," he said, "and for two pins I'd do it."

"Frank," I said, "don't be foolish. Don't go, if you feel like that. Wire them that you're ill. We'll talk about it to-morrow. I'll meet you anywhere you like."

"I'm nearly crazy with thinking. I can't go, and I can't stay either. I know what I ought to do all right, and I guess I'll do it."

"Frank!" I cried, but he had hung up the receiver. I made up my mind at once and fled upstairs and along to my room where I flung on a hat and a warm coat. I looked in my purse and saw I had just ten cents. In the hall I found the porter and asked him to lend me two dollars. With frightful slowness he counted it out and gave it to me, and I ran out of the front door, closing it softly after me, and down the snowy steps. I found a shabby hansom at the corner and got in. It was the first time in my life, I remember, that I had taken a cab at my own expense and alone. It had not occurred to me to ask my mother to come with me. In all such matters I acted for myself and by myself, then and always, and had no confidantes.

Frank was staying in a small hotel to be near his parents who had a tiny apartment in the next street. They knew as little of his movements as my mother knew of mine, and they had already preceded him to Boston. I knew the number of his room, for he had happened to mention it, so I got into the elevator and no one questioned me, for which I was thankful. If they had asked me my business there I should not have known how to answer. I reached the door unmolested, found it unlocked, and went in. For a moment my blood seemed to freeze. He was lying sprawled on the bed, face-downwards, but as I closed the door behind me he moved, looked round, and sprang up.

"Frank," I whispered. His face looked white and his eyes were swollen. He flung his arms about me, and we stood in silence, cheek to cheek. His suit-case and trunk were locked and ready. His watch lay on a small table by the bed, and beside it was a revolver. He must have felt me start, for he said: "It's all right. It isn't loaded—yet. The cartridges are in the drawer."

I saw that he was going to need managing and that I was in the midst of a most unhappy adventure, and I quailed, but suddenly the conviction came to me that I was stronger than he was and that I could make

46

him do anything I wanted. I pushed him away from me and said:

"Well, I'll tell you what I'll do, Frank. I'll keep that revolver till I see you again, and if you still want it I promise you I'll give it back."

I went to the table and picked it up, and he made no effort to stop me. I was not unaccustomed to these small, evil weapons, for my father had once taught me how to shoot and how to load and unload them. I saw that he had told me the truth. It was not loaded. I slipped it into the pocket of my coat.

"All right," he said dully. "Keep it if you like. I don't care what happens to me now."

"I do," I said briskly. "Did you send that telegram?"

"No. It's too late. They won't get it till the morning, anyway."

I looked at his watch. It was half-past eight and his train left at half-past nine.

"There's plenty of time to catch your train, and that's what you're going to do."

"Yes, I guess I am," he said wearily and sank down on the bed. "Mama, I darned nearly did it. I believe I would have if it had been loaded, but I just couldn't make up my mind to get off the bed and take the cartridges out of that drawer."

I went to the dressing-table, pulled open the top drawer and collected the cartridges that were roll-

47

ing about in it. These, too, I put into my pocket.

"Are you all ready?"

"Yes."

"It's snowing again and it may take you longer to get to the station than you think. Let's go down and tell them to send up for your things." As he made no movement, I said: "Come on, Frank. I can't stay long, you know. I just slipped out and if I'm missed there'll be awful trouble, and I've got troubles enough." My father had just written that he had failed to sell his invention and was coming home. My mother was in great distress of mind, as we had hardly any money. I told him this, adding: "I had to borrow two dollars from the porter to get here."

"Oh, Marna, you poor darling kid." He put his hand in his pocket and offered me two dollars, which I took, as I knew it would please him. "God, what a beast I was to make you come. It seemed as though I just had to see you again before I went—by train or —the other way."

"Well, now that you have," I said, "come along. And thank your lucky stars you aren't going to spend the rest of your days in boarding-houses and hotels, as I guess I'll have to do."

"No you won't, Marna. You'll marry some fellow with money who isn't as weak as I am. Oh, I know I'm weak, as weak as hell, don't imagine I don't know

48

it. Only I love you so awfully. Kiss me for the last time."

I took no pleasure in that kiss. I wanted to get the whole affair over now as soon as possible. I was desperately sorry for him, but it was his weakness I pitied more than himself, and love, with me, had little to do with pity. Though I could easily pity where I already loved I could never love what I first pitied, and I had never loved him. We walked down four flights of stairs, arm in arm, and I could feel his resolution coming back to him. By the time he was ready to go I knew that all was well. He put me into my waiting hansom, and I leaned over the folding doors and said:

"Frank, I believe you're going to be very happy. I can't tell you why I think it, but I do. I almost know it."

He sprang up on the step and kissed me, and we started off. I went away out of his sight and out of his life. He never claimed the revolver, and if he had he would not have got it, for I could not keep it, and sold it the next day in a pawn-shop in Twenty-First Street. The cartridges I dropped that night in a pile of snow. I got home without being missed, and when my mother came upstairs she found me reading *Amos Judd.*

I never saw a picture of Frank Bellamy's, and I never heard of any that he painted, though I asked

49

dealers in Paris and New York, and looked for his name in many an exhibition catalogue. But years after I saw in a newspaper that a Mr. and Mrs. Frank Bellamy were staying at the Ritz Hotel in Paris on their way to Venice, with their two children, Marna and Paul.

CHAPTER IV

I

 KEPT a diary which in those days was less a careful record of events than a chronicle of states of mind. On my twentieth birthday I wrote in it:

THINGS I ENJOY MOST:
1. Meeting and talking to men. (I suppose I mean having men like me.)
2. Nature, especially trees.
3. Literature. (*a*) Poetry (*b*) Prose.
4. Painting.
5. Travel. (Abroad. I am tired of this continent.)

I was very well informed about trees and flowers, and this knowledge, unlike other sorts, seemed to come to me without effort. I knew the wild flowers within reach of New York as I had known those of California and Oregon, while for trees I always had a feeling of intimacy and knew the different kinds at a glance, in winter or summer. I looked forward to spring with passion, and when it came, like many

51

another longing soul, I was restless and dissatisfied. My troubles, which had lain dormant in the winter, seemed to multiply like plants and put forth branches, but I nevertheless continued to long for it each year with increasing intensity. A recurring nightmare of mine, which psycho-analysts would doubtless find it easy to interpret nowadays, was of suddenly discovering that that for which I had waited with such ardour had come and gone without my knowledge, and I was aghast and heart-sick to find the leaves already brown and withered on the trees. I had somehow missed the spring, it had slipped by without me, and I would wake in anguish. Then I would remember that the lilac buds, those fore-runners of the great green miracle, were just breaking, that the whole lovely pageant of spring was still before me, and deeply comforted and reassured I would sleep again.

Admirers of no importance came and went. I cannot remember their faces now. They were an audience for me and as a means of expression and escape I valued them. With girls I felt shy and ill at ease.

My father's affairs had taken a turn for the better. He had sold his last invention outright and to fairly good advantage, and I now went to an art school every day from nine till four. We had a tiny apartment in Hundred-and-fourth Street that winter, with a coloured maid-of-all-work named Opal, and I never

went out without a feeling of guilt at leaving my
mother alone and lonely. She was ready to make
friends with such pleasant and friendly folk as were
near at hand, but she dropped them as soon as she
could no longer see them without effort. She now
relied entirely upon me for companionship, and I
know I was unsatisfactory, for I was silent and
dreamy. I often came home and found her crying,
and her unhappiness was like a fog on my youthful
spirits.

In the studio I was another creature. I had considerable talent for painting, and while I had always
known I could draw, I was unprepared for the praise
and interest my instructors accorded me. Mr. Cullen
Cobbes was particularly encouraging, and soon pro-
moted me to the joys of colour and canvas.

When I was twenty-four an English aunt of my
mother died and left her a small legacy. We had
no near relations in America at all, both my parents
being only children, and this sum coming as it did
from someone we had never seen, was divinely unexpected and welcome. It immediately sent my father's
ideas and hopes soaring, and as he had lately contrived, for the first time in his life, to put by something like twenty-five hundred dollars, he made up his
mind that we must go abroad. I think both he and
my mother felt they owed it to me. They realized
how small and poor had been my opportunities, and

that it was only through blind chance that I ever met anyone at all. In New York our tiny fortune would have melted like an icicle in a blow furnace and nothing would have been accomplished thereby, but in Paris or London it could be made to go a long way. And both my father and mother loved Paris and had the happiest recollections of it, for they had been young there, and well-to-do—it was before my father put everything he had into a Mexican mining venture and lost it—and life had seemed gay and rosy and promising. My father had a friend in Paris whom he had not seen or heard from for twenty years, and to whom I think he wished to put forward some scheme or other. My mother pointed out that he might be dead, but my father would not hear of it. They also thought it desirable to seek out my mother's English relations and introduce me to them, at the same time expressing their appreciation of that timely legacy. So on a wave of quite unreasoning optimism we prepared for the voyage. I bid the reproachful Mr. Cobbes good-bye—I was his best pupil that year and he was loth to see me go—and packed my painting materials in the bottom of my trunk together with four books of poetry and a bundle of love-letters. They helped to fill it, for I had few clothes and bought little for the journey.

If I crossed the Atlantic a hundred times no trip would ever again be as vivid, as remarkable as that

one. It was an escape from everything that had irked
and confined me. It seemed to wash out the boarding-houses, our cramped apartment and the slovenly
Opal, the years of poverty—and poverty in the midst
of the flaunting luxury of New York is double poverty—our neighbours with their commonplace minds,
the restrictions of my life. I only regretted the
studio. Now I was as excited and eager as a dog
loose in a forest. I felt, for the first time in my
adult life, that I suffered under no handicaps or dis-
advantages. It was true that my clothes were inadequate and shabby, but in those days I could rise above
such trifles and could wear rags and forget them.

It was inevitable, I suppose, that I should meet on
that boat a man who interested me and influenced my
life. I say inevitable because one was due. There
had been no one since Frank Bellamy who had been
more than a unit in a dim procession.

I was ripe, therefore, for fresh adventure, and,
as usual, one came to me without effort on my part.

My mother and father, when things were going
well, were very happy together, and on the lee-side
of fortune my mother basked prettily and delight-
fully in his admiration and love. They now left me
to walk and sit contentedly by myself, relieved for
the present of every care.

I had several times noticed—it would have been
difficult not to notice him—a tall, big-boned man in

a purplish-blue overcoat that reached to his heels. He was alone on the ship and few people spoke to him. His faded-looking hair and moustache were turning grey, and his expression was preoccupied and sad with that inner sadness which is not necessarily related to events. I felt sure he was English, for no one but an Englishman, I believed, could so confidently wear that remarkable overcoat. He had a fine, bold nose, high and authoritative, but the rest of his face, which was gentle, seemed to wish to efface this dominating effect. He sat at the Captain's table, and once when I passed close to his deck chair I saw that the book that lay open on his knees was the Bible, and that he was reading Proverbs.

I began to be curious about him, but nothing seemed less likely than that my curiosity would ever be satisfied. Sometimes I thought I saw him glance at me, and I wondered why. I had no good opinion of my personal attractions—though I had a secret and unfounded belief that I was somehow worth knowing—and this flicker of interest on his part surprised and flattered me.

On the morning of the third day he said good-morning to me as we passed each other on deck, and I returned the greeting, colouring and unable to conceal my startled confusion. It was so totally unexpected that my heart rapped wildly in silly turmoil.

"How absurd!" I said to myself. "It's quite right

and usual for people to speak on a ship. How stupid to blush and stammer." But I knew that in a few minutes we would meet again, and I suddenly made up my mind that I could not face it. What should I do? Smile at him or look the other way? I did not know, and the problem drove me, in cowardice and indecision, to the rail to stare out at the sea till he had passed. But he did not pass. He was suddenly beside me. The hand that rested on the rail held a Bible, and the face he turned towards me was, in a curious way, one of the most charming and immediately likeable that I have ever seen.

"What lovely colours!" he said, looking at the waves. The sun had just come out, and the water where it was flung away from the ship's sides and on the crests of the waves was ice-green, and in the troughs of the waves it was gentian blue.

"I should like a velvet suit," he went on, unexpectedly, "the colour of the crests of those waves." I laughed at this and he added: "With ruffles of yellowish, Mechlin lace."

"How beautiful that sounds. What a pity men can't wear the colours they like."

"Yes," he answered, "colours are like drugs to me. That was a charming red dress you wore last night."

I was amazed at this. He had noticed that old red velvet dress my mother and I had made two years ago. Ingenuously I told him its history.

"It was a very good colour, and suited you. What are you reading on the voyage? I have just been re-reading Proverbs and the book of Job. Job is particularly fine. Do you know the Bible well?"

"Not as well as I ought to," I said. "There's so much else to read."

"Yes. Still, I go back to it now and again with great pleasure."

"I would rather read other things," I said. "Philosophy for instance."

I was speaking to a man who had read and studied every philosophy from Socrates to William James. His eyes lit up with amusement and interest.

"What philosophy have you read?"

"A little Plato," I told him, "a little Bacon, a little Nietzsche."

"Then you are already a pessimist?"

"Yes," I answered, "I think I am."

"Tell me why. And tell me why, at your age, you read philosophy. What made you decide to be a pessimist?"

I said: "I think it's a matter of temperament, don't you? And I haven't had a very happy life. In fact, I've had hardly any life at all yet. I've had a great deal of time to think and wonder—and despair."

To no woman could I have made such an admission, for with women I was reserved and on the defensive. I suspected a critical, appraising attitude of mind in them, while in men I was only aware of an interest and friendliness that encouraged me to be frank. I imagined that women compared me unfavourably with themselves, as I compared myself unfavourably with them. I always supposed they had had advantages that I had not; that they had access to certain kinds of knowledge denied to me. I was without coquetry, and I think it was the easy coquetry I observed in most women that aroused my envy. I could neither feel it nor assume it, and when I tried I felt self-conscious and clumsy.

"What has been wrong with your life?" he asked. "You look as though you were possessed of every good."

"I think," I told him with careful accuracy, "that I have a sort of inner happiness that comes probably from youth and good health. It's when I compare myself with the idea I have in my mind of what I want to be, or with other people, that I'm miserable. I'm dissatisfied with everything then."

"Now that we've begun this interesting talk," he said, "we must go and sit down. Come, there's an empty chair next to mine."

Before the morning was over I had told him a good deal of my history, and he had begun to tell me his when the gong sounded for lunch. His name I now knew. He was a distinguished member of one of those famous English political families with whose

names even I was familiar. When he told me I felt
a little shock of awe and excitement go through me.
Why had he bothered to speak to me? I longed to
ask him.

It is difficult, indeed, as I look back to know what
it was that drew that sad, gentle, learned, sensitive
man toward me, but drawn he was from the first, as
I was drawn to him. I was so struck by the strange-
ness of it that I began to record in my diary the things
he said to me, the way our friendship ripened and
my feelings about him.

He had married at twenty-four a beautiful girl
with whom he had been in love during the whole of
his boyhood. She gave birth to a child which died,
and she contracted that rare illness that ends in insanity and of which I had never heard until he told
me of it, for I was woefully uninstructed in such
things. She was still alive, still hopelessly and pa-
thetically insane, and his life had been made hate-
ful to him by one of the worst tragedies that can be-
fall a human being.

Surely I was fortunate in my first Englishman!
With him I entirely put away all that lightly passionate and amorous side of me that made me greedy
for kisses and adoration. It might never have existed. In fact, when I was with him I wondered if I
could be the same girl who had ached for Frank Bellamy's caresses and for those of young men for whom

I had cared even less. I cannot invent a name for him, his own was so utterly right and expressed him so perfectly, so I will call him Richard, the one of his Christian names that I liked best, and which I soon learned to use.

I introduced him to my parents, and my mother showed the pleasure she felt at meeting this distinguished person. I made haste to tell her he was married and his wife insane, thereby dashing the first definite hope that had sprung in her breast in regard to me since Sanford's day. Nevertheless, she saw what an extraordinarily useful and devoted friend I had made and her face shone with satisfaction and pride. Richard saw all this, and in his human and lovable way was pleased by her ingenuousness. I think he understood and was charitable toward all human frailties—until his own feelings were too deeply involved and his sensitive nature too racked by them.

My financial prospects seemed to him precarious and unsatisfactory.

"But I expect to earn money," I told him.

"How? With your painting? And how soon can you hope to do that?"

I did not know, so he told me, and while it was discouraging I think it was good for me. In those days before the War the prospect of the young unknown artist was far less rosy even than it is to-day. He

61

himself bought modern pictures not because he liked them—he frankly and I think mistakenly did not—but because he thought it the right thing to do, and because it was, from the speculative point of view, amusing. It was the only form of speculation that appealed to him.

That famous old statesman, his father, was dead, and he lived with his older brother at a great country place, about forty miles from London. He said that I must come and stay, and I said that I would love it, and wondered if he could possibly mean it.

"I will arrange it with your mother," he said.

People looked at us and wondered, as for six days —it was one of the slower boats—we were continually together. A certain stout, ungainly woman I had seen him speak to once or twice was angry with him for not playing bridge with her. She had counted on him to make a fourth from New York to Liverpool, and she chid him one day in my presence for disappointing her. I was standing beside him when she came up and I was about to slip away when he caught my arm.

"This is my young friend, Marna Lattimer, Edith, from New York. She hopes to conquer fame with her brush. Marna, this is Lady Shalford."

She acknowledged the introduction without a gleam of interest and returned to the attack.

"But General Bray commits every crime known to

bridge players. You really must come to the rescue.
There's no one else on the ship one knows."

He arranged to play with her that evening, and we
moved away.

"A bun to the tiger," he whispered when we were
out of earshot. "That's a very offensive woman, and
I introduced you because it will be pleasant to have
you share my distaste. She is equally rude to anyone
not of her own immediate circle, so don't take her
snub personally. On the other hand, her husband is
a charming fellow, and my brother's greatest friend,
so you see my position."

I said I saw it perfectly well, but that I thought
most women were like that.

"They make me feel a miserable, crawling little
worm," I said. "No man has ever looked at me like
that, no, never, never. I don't like women. I've told
you so before. I hate them."

He scolded me. He said I would sing a very different tune some day, that women were better friends
to one another than—with rare exceptions—men ever
were to women, though he hoped it would be a long
time before I learnt this from experience.

I refused to believe it.

"I've had no friends among girls at all, and lots
among men."

"Friends? People who put your good before any
purposes of their own? Honest carers for your wel-

fare and happiness? Stop and think how many."

I stopped and thought. I could only think of Sanford as approximating to this ideal, and he had left me, knowing my dependence on him, because he valued his own peace of mind above everything.

"Anyway I like men better. I always shall."

"Like both, discriminatingly, and love very few."

"I only mean to love one," I said, with the sentimental optimism of youth.

"How well I remember saying that at twenty!" he told me. "Do you know George Meredith's *Love in the Valley*? If you do, that is what I felt for Florence, my wife. A romantic, exalted, passionate adoration that utterly possessed me. She was the loveliest thing I have ever seen." As we walked the deck he quoted:

"Stepping down the hill with her fair companions,
    Arm in arm, all against the raying West,
Boldly she sings, to the merry tune she marches,
    Brave is her shape, and sweeter unpossessed.
Sweeter, for she is what my heart first awaking
    Whispered the world was; morning light is she.
Love that so desires would fain keep her changeless;
    Fain would fling the net, and fain have her free."

He repeated, " 'Sweeter unpossessed,' " and stared at the horizon with tragic eyes.

64

"Yes, I know that poem. I've known it for years.
I'll read it again," I said, "thinking of you."

Head thrown back as he walked, with half-closed
eyes, he went on:

"Happy, happy time, when the white star hovers
  Low over dim fields fresh with bloomy dew,
Near the face of dawn, that draws athwart the
    darkness,
  Threading it with colour, like yewberries the yew.
Thicker crowd the shades as the grave East deepens
  Glowing, and with crimson a long cloud swells.
Maiden still the morn is; and strange she is and
    secret;
    Strange her eyes; her cheeks are cold as cold
    sea-shells."

Somehow those verses told me, as nothing else
could, what she had been to him, what she was like,
and how the tragedy had fallen upon them. It
touched me, and for a moment I put my hand in his.

"Ah, well, all that was more than twenty years ago.
I'm forty-eight now, Marna, and I've loved other
women. Don't think me a saint or an æsthete. I am
neither. But she goes with me wherever I go:

"Borne to me by dreams, when dawn is at my eye-lids,
  Fair as in the flesh she swims to me on tears."

65

Then abruptly he changed the subject.

"How I wish I had known you in New York! I was a week there and saw only official folk. Do you know why I have been to Japan? Would it interest you to know? "

I said that it would, exceedingly, and he told me. He had gone there on an errand for the British Foreign Office, and he explained to me its objects and results. All this would be made public upon his arrival in England, but at that moment no one knew of it outside official circles. He told me many amusing and interesting things about Japan and his visit there. I was enthralled, entranced by him, by his whole personality, his odd and delightful character, and above all by his curious and sudden attachment to me. He would sometimes seek out my mother and talk to her about me, asking her questions about my childhood and praising me without stint.

"I wish he hadn't got that poor little wife," my mother said. "If he hadn't, would you marry him? "

Such questions annoyed me by their futility, but they set me thinking. If he had not, would I, supposing that he asked me? I knew that, in spite of all he could give me, I would not. I was waiting for something very different. My mother liked to play with the idea of a good marriage for me, but she was no schemer—nor was I. She, like myself, was too innocent, too unworldly and too sentimental. She believed

66

that "Mr. Right," that obliging, ubiquitous, mythical gentleman so consoling to mammas of her calibre and period would inevitably find me out. As for my father, he saw no reason at all why I should not remain their unmarried daughter for ever, and was jealous of every male comer.

We were to spend a few days in London to make ourselves known to my mother's relations and were then to proceed to Paris. Richard would also be in London, and he made plans for me. He would take me out to dinner, to the theatre, to the Zoo. He would arrange for me to meet his brother, his sister-in-law, who would love me, he was sure—I was not sure at all—but it was delightful to be thus thought of and planned for. My mother asked him in her ingenuous way if he knew her relations, who lived in Putney, and he gravely said he was sorry he did not.

The night before we left the ship Richard talked to me very seriously. He said I must be very careful of myself in Paris, that Frenchmen were too enterprising where young women were concerned and that I must be continually on my guard.

"Your mother," he said, " is a dear thing, but she doesn't in the least know how to take care of you. And your father will only be thinking about business."

"Oh, I've always looked after myself," I told him.

"And I'm quite able to, I assure you. I know more about men than you think."

"You know a good deal about nice men," he said. "I'm not saying there are not nice Frenchmen. There are, of course, but you'll be extremely likely to meet undesirable ones, I'm afraid, particularly if you go to an art school. I want you to be more circumspect, even, than you think you need to be. My dearest Marna, I care so very much what happens to you."

My spirits suddenly sank and I felt forlorn and depressed. What he was saying was so true. I was so at the mercy of chance.

"Oh, nothing that means anything that leads anywhere ever happens to me!" I cried.

"Doesn't this mean anything? Do you think this won't lead anywhere?"

I was afraid I had hurt him, for I had already observed his sensitiveness.

"But I'm losing you so soon. That's just what I complain of. You'll go out of my life just as suddenly as you came into it."

"I will never go out of your life," he told me with great earnestness, "until you wish me to. Please remember that."

And within a few days I was nearly to throw away the only perfect and disinterested friendship I have ever had with a man.

68

II

Richard was the only being I have ever known who was always the same, whether he were talking to a waiter or a cabinet minister. His suave, charming manner never altered, the gentle and kindly expression of his face never changed. I have often—alas!—seen him hurt, but never angry. He had friends everywhere, and when I went out with him in London we were constantly meeting them, and he always took the trouble to introduce them to me in some particularly pleasing way. It did not take me long to discover that he was not at all in the habit of conducting young women about, or showing any great interest in them, and he told me I was the first friend of my age, state and sex he had made since his own youth.

Those first few days in London were almost entirely absorbed by him. It was early May, and I shall never forget the impression London made on me. The air was warm and still, the trees everywhere were burgeoning out into leafy roundness and fulness. The fronts of the houses were gay with fresh paint and flowers. The traffic rumbled along the wooden paving blocks of the streets with a duller, more subdued note than I was used to. The "season," which meant nothing to me, was in full swing, and I caught glimpses of men in wonderful uniforms, of cocked hats and plumes and feathers, of swords and gold braid, and of gaily-dressed women. All this was stirring and exciting to me. I had no wish to take part in these things, only to observe them and to hear about them from Richard.

We stayed in rooms near Dorest Square that had been recommended to my mother by someone on the boat, and had two bedrooms and a sitting room. Our relations in Putney were away, and were not returning for four or five days, so we made up our minds to stay on in London for another week, and I, of course, was happy enough to do so.

On Thursday—we had arrived on a Monday— Richard came to tell me that he had arranged for me to go down to Bolsover House to stay with his brother and sister-in-law from Friday to Monday. It was the first week-end invitation I had ever had, and it threw me into a sort of panic. Richard soothed all my nervous fears and my mother's anxieties about clothes with a few words. We were not to fuss. His sister-in-law was a plain woman who cared nothing for dress. I would think her the dowdiest of the dowdy. His brother, he was sure, I should find the least alarming of men, and there would be no one else there except their son, his nephew from Sandhurst, a nice boy. We should be out of doors all day. I should need a pair of country shoes, a plain frock for the day, and an evening dress. My red one would look magnificent. I could have hugged him for this adorable understanding of our problems. He said he would call for me the next afternoon at three, and we would go by train.

When he had gone my mother immediately thought of the nephew from Sandhurst. How lovely if he should be a charming young man and fall in love with me! It seemed to her that Providence was taking me under its downiest wing. My father, on the other hand, asked me questions that made me laugh.

"How do you know it's all right, and that the sister-in-law will really be there? What do you know about them, anyway? It seems to me they're rushing you off your feet. Don't you cheapen yourself by jumping at any and every invitation that comes your way."

He fussed and blustered and my mother scolded him and took him away, leaving me to darn and mend and overhaul my few clothes in peace.

A Daimler car met us at the country station the next day and we were driven through the most exquisite country I had ever seen. Oh, English fields, English lanes in May, who, having once seen you can ever forget you, can ever cease to love you? If there is a heaven perceptible to those senses we now have, surely it will be made of springy, English turf, on which hawthorn trees, foaming with scented bloom, will drop their small petals: surely great spreading

71

limes and beeches with pale, translucent foliage of
shining green piled mountain-high, will fold the cattle
under their deep shade. So I thought that day, so I
shall always think.

A great park, a great house of grey stone, immense
lawns, men-servants, a vast, high hall with banners
hanging from a balcony, Richard being divested of
the long, purplish overcoat and saving me, with a
look, from panic, a walk through room after room,
all seeming to me magnificent, till we reached a door
opening on more lawns and trees, and there we saw
a tea-table spread with a white cloth and silver, and
three people rising to their feet as we appeared.

Richard's brother, greyer and stouter, came forward and I met him first; his wife, standing at the
tea-table, was as Richard had described her—homely
in the English sense, plain, yet very impressive none
the less, and lastly there was a young man in flannels,
and I saw the object of my first wild, short-lived un-
thinking passion, even as I took his hand.

He was the most beautiful thing I had ever seen. I
was half afraid to look at him, yet looked again and
again with quick, observing glances. I knew enough
from my studies to realize that here was a body to
have inspired a Praxiteles. He was very fair, with a
skin as white as milk except where the sun had
touched it. He had a small, new, fair moustache as
golden as his hair, regular features, eyes of brightest

72

blue and a mouth and expression of great charm and sweetness. I had never dreamed of anything so beautiful (and so *moving* as he was in his beauty) in my life.

I talked to the others, but I was conscious of him all the time. Richard's sister-in-law asked me numbers of questions about America, and I soon saw that she was not at all a clever woman, merely capable and energetic. His brother was very different. He seemed to me to have that natural understanding and clarity of mind that Richard had himself—that men have so much oftener than women, I think—and although I tried to like her and to make her like me, I did not feel drawn to her in any way. I felt that her mind was full of laundry lists and other necessary, tiresome, domestic details. We sat there talking, David, the son, saying the least, till the shadows lay in long parallel lines across the grass, and the birds' clamour increased with the approach of sundown. Then I was taken round the garden, and saw wistaria vines hundreds of years old embracing high brick walls, their thousand arms dripping with mauve blossoms. It was all lovely, all enchanting to me. What lives these people led, I thought, like gods and goddesses! Only later did I understand how they paid for all this beauty by unending dull duties unquestioningly performed—duties it tired my mind to think about.

Sixteen to Forty

I was shown to a chintz-hung room where I found my poor possessions laid away in great lavender-scented drawers and cupboards as though they had belonged to a princess. I looked with shame at my worn, wooden hair-brush, at my cheap celluloid hand mirror. I bathed and put on my red dress and went downstairs without waiting for a gong, for I was fearful of being late. I found David already dressed, reading and smoking in the drawing-room. He sprang up as I came in, and again I felt that sharp spasm of wonder and admiration. How lovely he was! I had not dreamed a man could be so perfect. He suggested that we go out on the terrace, and as I had not a wrap he removed a great square of old brocade from the piano and threw it round me. He told me about his life at Sandhurst and said that he was just finishing there and was soon to go to India. He made me think of the Brushwood Boy in his young uprightness and perfection, and I wished passionately that I were Miriam, at the same time yearning over him with the feelings of a mother. I envied his mother; I envied his some-time wife; I envied all the women he might ever love.

We played bridge that evening, David and Richard cutting in. When David played I made mistakes, unable to keep my mind on the game, but when Richard was there I played steadily and well.

The next day we walked, Richard, David and I, all

over the estate, and I picked my first cowslips and
saw my first wild hyacinths. David and Richard
talked a great deal together about the trip to Japan
and all that had happened there and about affairs
in Ireland and India, and I listened, happy that they
felt they could be quite natural with me.

On Sunday we went to church. The church was on
the estate, and I sat in the family pew, wondering
at the strange chance that had brought me there.
David had told me that he liked singing the hymns,
and I listened to his charming voice worshipfully.
A kind of intimacy had sprung up between us. We
were naturally drawn together, I suppose, by our
youth and by our common attitude toward life, which
was one of expectancy. My American accent was a
great joy to him, and he said it was a new experience
to meet an American who was poor, as I assured him
I was. Richard told me how much they all liked me,
and it warmed my heart. It seemed that they liked
me for being simple, shy, and uncertain of myself,
even, I think, for being badly dressed. Richard's
thoughtfulness for me was without end. It was he
who knew how to present me to them in the most attractive and acceptable light, it was he who knew how
to put me at my ease with them all, it was his liking
for me and his odd pride in me that gave me sub-
stance and a background, and such was the fascina-

tion David had for me that I came near to forgetting all this and nearer still to losing it.

I had never heard a nightingale, and David's father told him to take me out to see if they were performing that evening. The others showed no disposition to follow us, though I knew afterwards that Richard, with his delicate restraint, was waiting for me to suggest that he should come too. I did not suggest it. I was too stirred and thrilled by the idea of going alone with David. He took me along the terrace to the end where we looked away to the lake down a wide grassy avenue cut through the woods. We thought we heard bird notes, so delicately etched on the silence that we could not be sure.

"We'll go nearer," said David, "if you're sure you're not going to be cold."

I assured him that I was warm enough, and we walked down that grassy avenue side by side. I knew for the first time what it was like to be almost fainting with love. My longings included no more than a kiss, no more than to be held, for a few seconds, in his arms, and I think I would have died for it that night. We went on, softly, and presently we heard what we had come to hear, that silver, bubbling, exquisite sound, like notes sung under water. I was entranced. For a long time we listened in silence, hardly breathing, then David made a little sudden movement, and touching my arm, whispered:

Sixteen to Forty

"We must go back."

I remember putting my hand up to my throat as though my heart were beating there, and our eyes met in the moonlight. His beauty was almost terrible and, alarmed at the tumult it aroused in me, I walked quickly toward the house and went up the shallow, grassy steps of the terrace. But he knew well enough what I was feeling, for he, too, was struggling with the same sharp want. Following me, a step or two below me, he caught me round the waist and drew me to him, and I looked down into his upturned face and beseeching upturned eyes.

"Shall I ever see you again?" he whispered, and suddenly put his head, that shining, lovely head against my breast. I held it there in an ecstasy I had never known before, then moved slowly down a step, two steps, to his level. My arms went round his neck and his went round my waist and we kissed. I could no more have helped it than I could have helped drawing my breath. It was the first really lyric kiss I had ever known. It was the very expression of myself at a moment of rapture.

There was a sound on the terrace, perhaps a door opening, and we sprang apart, and, without a word, walked back to the house. I do not know how long we had been gone, five minutes or two hours, though I think it was nearer the first, but as soon as I looked at Richard's face I knew that he either thought I had stayed out too long or that he had seen. He was standing by the French window as we came in, and his face was strangely altered. His expression had become cold, formal, and a film seemed to cover his eyes.

"Well?" asked David's mother. "Any luck?"

"Oh, yes," I said. "They were wonderful. We walked as far as the edge of the woods. I think there must have been ten of them singing. I never heard anything so lovely." My knees were trembling, but I think I appeared composed. I looked meaningly at Richard. "I wish you had come, too."

"Ah, I've heard nightingales before," he said, but he did not look at me. His changed face cut me to the heart and I felt sick with dread. When it was time to go to bed he said good-night to me politely and coldly, the others warmly, saying it was a pity I had to leave them to-morrow. I went to my room thinking of suicide. In five minutes I had destroyed the greatest fortune, the finest gift that had ever come my way. My despair was black and unlit by any hope. I, who had so little, had thrown everything away. I sat at my mirror and looked at myself with streaming eyes.

To kiss David had seemed so right, so necessary; to hurt Richard—but I had never meant to hurt him —was so terrible. I think I suffered from his hurt more even than he could have suffered himself. The

78

next morning I had no opportunity of speaking to him, for he was not coming to London that day.

"I'll write," I said, looking into his cold, estranged eyes. No one else saw that things had gone wrong. David, I know, thought our secret was ours for ever. I drove away, not knowing whether I were happy or miserable, whether my visit had been a success or a disaster. I feared the latter. But I had fallen wildly in love with David, and I knew that in all probability I should never see him again.

I have often wondered if that night we had not, both of us, some prescience of the future. He spent two years in India, returning to England in July, 1914. He went at once to France with the first Expeditionary Force and was blown to pieces during the retreat from Mons.

I think I have remembered a million times that night when he laid his shining head against my breast.

CHAPTER V

WEEK later we went to Paris.

We had seen the Lawtons—my mother's relations—several times. They were quiet folk with a sort of musty gentility about them and led unselfish, uneventful lives in their ugly house in Putney. I found them indescribably depressing. My mother admired their solid virtues and their solid silver, and my father admired old Mr. Lawton's shrewd business brain. He was a successful retired tea-merchant. They had long talks, while I was left with their pious, plain and ageing daughter Celia, and I was very glad when we saw them for the last time, for they were in every way antipathetic to me.

I did not see Richard again before I left, as he did not come to London, but a letter from him in answer to the one I wrote to him imploring his forgiveness, reached me in Paris, and completely restored me to my former place in his affections. I discovered that he had seen nothing, but that he was deeply wounded that I had not asked him to join us; he thought I had stayed out longer than I should—"But that was only my wretched jealousy . . ." he said, and that I liked

being with David more than being with him. I had
hurt him. I had made him feel old, I had seemed to
him ungrateful. "And yet God knows it isn't gratitude I want." I vowed to myself that I would never
offend again, and was supremely thankful that I had
not lost him for ever. I knew I should see him in
Paris before very long and, greatly comforted, I set
about adjusting myself to my new life.

We took a small furnished apartment off the Avenue Victor Hugo and engaged a stout, elderly "bonne
à tout faire." But a terrible disappointment had
come to my father, for his old friend, the only man
I have ever known him to speak of with affection, was
dead. He had died eight months before, and my
mother wisely and kindly refrained from saying, "I
warned you." I did not remember him, as I was a
mere baby when we left Paris, but his loss had the
strangest effect on my father, to whom death—his
own or other people's—was always a remote improb-
ability, and one which, in his optimism and his re-
fusal to face facts, he never visualized. It was evi-
dent that he had been picturing his old friend as he
had looked when they last met, more than twenty
years ago, and now all the zest and purpose seemed
to have gone out of this trip to Europe. He was
already feeling, I could see, that we had better not
have come, and wondering what he was to do next,
so I hastily hunted up an art school—I asked a pic-

ture dealer in the Avenue de l'Opéra for advice, as I knew no one—and he directed me to Monsieur Vacaire.

I knew that I could not and must not go back to New York and my old life there, that I must hold on to Paris for the present with determination, and I began to work feverishly at my painting, like a man who makes speed to build a raft when he sees the floods are coming.

Old Monsieur Vacaire was a seedy intellectual who had studied under Manet, and he often told us of the time of the Great Exhibition of 1867 when Manet's Execution of the Emperor Maximilian was prohibited by the authorities from being hung. Monsieur Vacaire had taught in London and spoke quite good English, which was lucky for me, as I knew almost no French. I soon picked up enough at the studio to make myself understood. There were only fifteen pupils in all, and only a certain number of these came every day. There were seven men of various ages and nationalities and the rest were all Frenchwomen and girls, with the exception of myself and a Miss Steevens who came from the North of England. She was the first woman friend I ever had, and she at once took me under her wing. She was a suffragette and an anarchist (or so she said), and the contrast between the extreme violence of her views and the extreme gentleness and goodness of her actions always amused and delighted me. She lived in Paris the life of a virtuous English spinster. She might have been living in a Cathedral town where her every action could be watched, and yet mentally she was the most broad-minded, unconventional woman I have ever known. She believed in free love and the abolition of marriage, and trembled when any of the male members of the class showed me any special attention—which was really seldom enough, for in the studio, at least, we were a sexless band.

My father was now trying to do some business with the French Government through a man named Sylvestre, whom he had met years ago. Sylvestre seemed to think he might be able to persuade the French Government to buy a kind of collapsible camping outfit my father had once devised and patented in America. It was intended for the use of boys at military schools or for troops during manœuvres. The moment Sylvestre took an interest in it my father considered the thing as good as done, and bought my mother a new ring.

"Both Sylvestre and I will do well out of this," he said. "The French Government can use hundreds of thousands of those outfits."

But there were many important men he or Sylvestre would have to meet and talk to, and these were invariably difficult to get at. If, after weeks of waiting, they should succeed in getting an appointment, they would find a mere underling or someone who opposed the idea. So time went by; August came, and my parents went to the sea-side and I went with Miss Steevens to the country to paint. Autumn and winter came, and my father was still optimistic. I think, as I look back, that he was one of the strangest men I have ever known. Only the future existed for him, and it would be as he wished. The present was so unimportant as to be undeserving of notice. He was never ill and never suffered pain, so I think there was nothing insistent enough to drag him back to the actual *now*. He thought my mother's anxieties silly. If our circumstances were unsatisfactory at the moment—and he would not admit that they were, for we had food and a roof over our heads—we had only to look ahead where everything good awaited us. He was unconscious of the passing of time, and delays that would have driven most men crazy he seemed not to notice at all.

Meanwhile, although I was in most ways as badly off as I had been in New York and led a lonely life and met no one, I was far happier than I had ever been before.

Richard came to Paris twice, and when he was there I lived in a sort of dream. He had a charming gift of making one feel rare, unique, of superior quality, and this almost compensated me for the poor opinion I had of myself at other times. I longed for

84

his comings and they seemed to obliterate the months in between. He saw my work and was impressed, and bought the first picture I ever sold—a painting of a street in the village on the Loire where I had spent my holiday.

A picture, like a poem, is an emotional crisis; the result of a moment of intense vision, or intense feeling. I was always in love when I painted, in love with that which I painted, and I strove with a kind of anguish to possess it, to make it mine for ever.

Richard said he knew no one in Paris but stiff, official people who moved in certain grooves, and who would not interest me.

"Except Edouard, my cousin. I wonder—I've often thought you might like him. I think he would make you laugh. Anyway, I'll ask him to lunch to meet you to-morrow."

An aunt of Richard's had married a Frenchman named Paul de Solieux, and Edouard was their son. Madame de Solieux had become entirely French, she even looked and thought like a Frenchwoman, he told me, and it would be difficult for me to imagine that Edouard had a drop of English blood in him. It was difficult. We lunched at La Rue's the next day, and I met him.

Edouard was my first Frenchman—not counting my fellow students, and I found him delightful. He was one of those stout men who move with exceeding

lightness and agility and have small, neat hands and
feet. I used to wonder if he were not full of air, so
buoyant and imponderable did he seem when he
moved. His face was round and smiling, and his
small dark eyes twinkled over his fat cheeks. He had
great charm, and an interesting mind, and spoke English, of course, perfectly, though he was sometimes
at a loss for a technical word. He was connected
with some bank—rather loosely, I think, as he seemed
to spend his days as he pleased—composed songs,
adored music, and played the 'cello.

He knew Vacaire and told me stories about him.

"He is said," he told me, "to have the honour of
being Ninon de l'Enclos' last lover, but, of course, I
don't swear to that."

I would not have Vacaire made fun of.

"He may be old, but he's an excellent teacher, and
he knows almost everything there is to know about
painting. I don't want to study with a fashionable
painter."

"Miss Lattimer is painting seriously, not for mere
amusement," said Richard. "Also she has very great
talent."

Edouard said he knew I had talent, and Richard,
suspecting a hollow compliment, asked him how he
knew.

"Because of the width between the eyes, and because she has not those useless, long, idle hands that

86

are called artistic and never accomplish anything, but square-palmed, capable hands, with short, strong fingers."

I held up my hands, palms out, delighted.

"I'll never be ashamed of them again!" I cried. "All my life I've kept them under tables and in the folds of my dresses, but I never will again."

"My dear," Richard protested, "surely I've told you that you have good hands. Do you only believe Edouard?"

He was hurt. That most sensitive man was hurt by this trifle.

"But Richard, you're so biased. You like everything about me simply because it's mine."

"That is so," he admitted, smiling.

We had a gay lunch and I found Edouard as easy as an old shoe; but I always felt comfortable at once with anyone Richard was fond of.

For a long time Paris meant Edouard to me, and London Richard. London meant a gentle, lovable man in a long overcoat, or perhaps an old and unfashionable suit that went none too well with the gay carnation in the button-hole—he loved carnations and they grew fine ones at Bolsover. It meant Richard's well-stored and cultivated mind, it meant lunches and dinners in the almost empty dining-rooms of old and dignified clubs, or in quiet restaurants where there

87

was no music—easier to find then than now. It meant shops where exquisite old silver was sold, which Richard would fondle and admire and sometimes rather shamefacedly buy, for he already had many treasures. And it meant the Zoo, and concerts, and the National Gallery. Paris meant the Louvre and the Musée Cluny with Edouard, the bridges of the Seine, old book-shops, conversation, discussions (Edouard talked to me more, I think, than any other man I have ever known. His talk was quite unceasing and nearly always amusing). And it meant restaurants where the food was rich and good.

With Richard I was an adoring little girl; with Edouard I was almost a woman of the world, a painter and an atheist.

For Edouard would admit nothing at all, not even a "mover that is moved," great admirer though he was of Aristotle. The universe was a combination of happenings, no more extraordinary, as happenings, than any others, but for Edouard extremely fortunate, as they had given him birth. I argued with him, feebly enough, trying to get him to admit the existence of some Cause or Force or God, but his wits and knowledge and skill in argument were too much for me, and I soon found myself on his side. He was a happy and good-natured hedonist. He loved the world as no one I have ever known has loved it, and with gusto. He loved crowds, cities, music, food, na-

ture (from a distance!), literature, ideas, physical
comforts and joys, perfumes, children, and women.
How he loved women! He had a mistress of whom
he often talked to me—never, of course, by name.
She was an Italian, separated from her husband, and
was older than Edouard, very experienced and very
seductive. He said she was both intellectual and
amorous.

"Marna, if you wish all men to love you, be like
her, in all but her misfortunes."

He talked to me as though I were forty, and I liked
it, though I often wondered if Richard would have
approved. But all the time he talked my mind was
busy accepting and discarding. Much that he said
I discounted as untrue, at least for me, but he succeeded in weakening, little by little, many of my Puri-
tan prejudices.

The Anglo-Saxon idea of feminine virtue incensed
him to the highest degree, and he made me ashamed
of all my small love affairs—not because they had
ended where they had, but because they had ever been
lightly embarked upon. I defended them all the
same.

Love was to him the loveliest thing in the world,
and was neither to be profaned nor belittled. He
thought it should have a kind of right-of-way through
the universe. It was the inspiration of all good, the
sum of all beauty. When I asked him to define it

89

he said it was the pleasure, mental and physical, that two people took in one another. I listened to him talking about love, music and philosophy for hours on end, but mostly love. When I compared myself with Miss Steevens I thought I knew or could imagine all there was to know about love. When I listened to Edouard I knew nothing whatever. But I also knew that it was not from him I wished to learn.

"I don't think Marna ought to be seeing so much of that Frenchman," my father said.

"Oh, nonsense!" my mother replied. "Why, Marna wouldn't have any pleasures at all if you had your way. She hasn't the money or the nice clothes to go out socially even if she knew people." Then she spoke of Richard. "Besides, that Frenchman, as you call him, is his cousin."

"That may be," my father said, "but one of these days Marna'll get mixed up in some sort of scandal if she doesn't look out. Somebody'll try to run off with her or something. You let her go around alone much too much."

My poor mother tried to explain how helpless she was.

"We can't do anything for her ourselves. And young men don't want a woman of my age about all the time."

She told me of this conversation—they had many like it—and I said:

"Oh, please don't worry about me, either of you. I'm quite able to take care of myself. I've never lived a conventional sort of life, and I wouldn't begin now if I could."

But in those days I secretly and bitterly regretted that I had no "background," no position, no home, no suitable friends, and that I had never "come out." I felt I had been cheated, and I think it was this feeling that drove me into seizing whatever pleasures I could find, and they, of course, were supplied by my male acquaintances.

I met Edouard's father and mother. Madame de Solieux always wore severe black, and she was excessively formal and "gratin." Her husband was even less human than she. I think they were the most stiff, cold, correct and bloodless beings it has ever been my lot to meet. They lived in the Faubourg, and adored Edouard fanatically. They highly disapproved of me, and not even Richard's friendship (friendship between a male and a female being always suspect) and Edouard's charming introduction could make me acceptable to them. I was a "jeune fille à marier," and as such was incorrect in every conceivable way. It was bad enough to go to an art school and paint from the nude. It was terrible to go about unchaperoned with men. They accepted the existence of Edouard's mistress without question or criticism. His innocent friendship with me shocked

91

them to the bone. I implored him never to let me see them again.

One day Edouard and I met at lunch at a small restaurant near the studio which was unknown to tourists and where the food was particularly good. I was late, and had washed and tidied myself hastily, and was looking and feeling shabby. Edouard did not in the least mind this. All his women friends were very much in society and unquestionably smart, and I think I provided an agreeable change for him.

As we were ordering lunch a fair-skinned, good-looking man came in alone, and looked for a table. Edouard at once hailed him, and they seemed well pleased to see one another, talking with great friendliness and the repeated use of "mon cher." Edouard introduced him to me and asked him to join us, which he did. He was the Comte de Rambaud, a Norman, and a very handsome man indeed. He showed traces of Viking blood in his bold features and bold blue eyes. He had a caressing voice, particularly when addressing a woman, that both repelled and attracted me. I thought he could probably create a temporary heaven for any woman who was looking for a heaven of that description, but I could feel about him, like a kind of miasma, the adoration of many of my sex, and it prejudiced me against him. I was as nearly rude as I could be to a man who was so little acquainted with the subtleties of the language he was

92

gallantly essaying. I could now make myself understood in French, but with this self-confident stranger
I preferred to speak in English, as it gave me an advantage over him that I felt I needed. He was not
interested as Edouard was in literature, in art and in
music, but only, I felt sure, in society, games and
women, and I disliked him for it.

As Edouard was greedy and liked to take time over
his meals—as did I when time did not matter—I had
a short lunch and went back to work, leaving the two
men together.

"How did you like de Rambaud?" he asked me
when I next saw him.

"He has all the French qualities I dislike, and you
have all the ones I like, Edouard," I said.

"Together then," he returned, with his rich laugh,
"we make one complete Frenchman." He added: "He
is brave, and though he has not a great brain he is
much liked. He seemed to find you interesting and
asked many questions, which I answered discreetly
when I answered them at all."

"I'm sure you answered them all, and volubly,"
I told him. "Of course he asked questions. I've
never known anything like the curiosity of the French
where women are concerned. What did you tell
him?"

"That you were a type he would not understand.
That your mind controlled and would always control

your emotions—this to show there was no chance for him. That you were well-balanced, fastidious, half woman, half child. That if you married, which, as you are both intellectual and critical, is unlikely, you would be conferring untold blessings on some probably unworthy but supremely fortunate man."

"I wonder which, if any, of those things you really did say."

"As you don't like him," he replied, "I don't think it matters."

I heard no more of de Rambaud till later, in February, and then in an unexpected way.

Miss Steevens had been ill. She narrowly escaped pneumonia, and for weeks was unable to come to the studio (which was only heated by an inadequate stove, and I suffered cruelly from colds and chilblains). When she got better the doctor ordered her south, and she begged me to go with her and offered to pay all my expenses. She was better off than the rest of us, for she had a small, reliable income that freed her from worry, and as she lived with careful economy, she was able to save. Certainly I could not have paid my own way. The "coup" with the French Government still hung fire, and nothing was settled. My father had other schemes on foot, but none that did not seem to me fantastically unlikely to come to anything. So once again our finances were dangerously low, and once again my poor mother had cause for the daily worry and uncertainty from which she had already suffered too much. I hated to leave her, her days were so empty. She was not interested in the things that interested me, and was terrified of the Paris streets. But I hoped to do some paintings that I might sell, and as the trip would cost nothing it seemed advisable to go.

We travelled third, of course, sitting up all night, and though I ached in every bone the next morning I was cheered by the sight of the sun, and by the strange, beautiful and extremely paintable scenery. We reached our destination late that afternoon. It was an old town about two miles from the coast and situated on a hill-top, like all the others, for safety from the Saracens and other invaders. Certainly I had not imagined that the South of France was so romantic and lovely, and I was delighted with everything I saw. In our village the houses leaned mysteriously together, making enchanting angles against the sky and deep shadows below, while the sun painted their sides and roofs in bright clear colours. Weather-beaten doors in old walls leapt to the painter's eye, and all about us were olive groves, the tender blue of distant hills, and below us the steady, aching blue of the Mediterranean. The farmhouse in which we had rooms was none too clean, and we were aware of that Italian smell that clings to the villages of the South of France, and seems made up of the smells of chickens, sour wine, onions, cheese and decay. Also there was no bath, and I looked longingly toward the sea, but they said it was too cold to bathe.

However, the sun made everything gay. Miss Steevens stayed at home for the first day or two, while I roamed about in search of subjects. The main village street occupied me first; narrow, dark, with pleasing doorways, and penetrated by patches of brilliant sunlight. At first I was surrounded by curious women and children, but they soon tired of me and went about their own affairs.

An occasional car passed, scattering the dogs and chickens, for our village seemed to lie between somewhere and somewhere, and they sometimes paused, but more often went by without slackening their speed. One day when I had nearly finished painting there I heard the far away snore of a powerful car, traveling fast. It came nearer with a noise that was an offence, but as it reached me it stopped. I turned my head and saw a long red and black monster, with fittings of shining brass. There were two people in it, a man and a woman, and I think the woman was curious to see what I was doing, for the man got out and examined the tyres in what seemed to me a perfunctory manner while she took off her veil and leaned out, the better to see. She was the loveliest woman, I think, that I have ever laid eyes on. She was dark—I think real beauty is always sombre, as is the greatest literature, and the greatest music—and she reminded me, with her exquisitely modelled face, of Leonardo's portrait of Lucrezia Crivelli in the Louvre. I could not help staring at her, and she half smiled at me—that half smile was so right, too, for that face—and draped her veil over her hat again. Her companion returned to his seat, and for the first time I saw his face. Our eyes met, and there was recognition in both. Then he looked quickly away and started the car, and I saw the colour surge into his face. He looked angry, annoyed, and in two seconds they were streaming along the road out of the village, leaving a long white plume of dust behind them.

It was certainly de Rambaud, and I thought the woman was, as far as looks were concerned, a very fit companion for him. He was evidently displeased at having been seen by me. Clearly he had an affair on foot and wanted no witnesses, and I made up my mind that, as I had seen him so accidentally, I would not speak of it to anyone, not even to Edouard.

We spent three weeks there, and were well pleased with our stay. Miss Steevens had stopped coughing, and it was time to go back to Paris. I had grown very fond of her and she was fiercely devoted to me. She wanted me to marry in good bourgeois fashion and have a family, and although she loved painting and it gave her an object in life, she was scornful of the part women played in art, and begged me not to

97

put it before everything else, as genius alone, and not mere talent, deserved this sacrifice. I was amused at her wish to see me married. It was so contrary to her views of life.

"Nothing that I say ever applies to you," she told me. "The ideas I express about life and morals are sincere, but they apply to the world as it *will be* and not as it is now. I preach them because I believe ideas are the most formative of all things, and it's through them that the world will be changed. But at present we must live in it, and as happily as we can."

Paris was bleak and bitter, the skies looked black to our eyes, and the unkind snow of March lay in the streets, a discouraging sight. I found things at home much as I had left them, or rather worse. My father had made no progress at all, and Sylvestre seemed to think he had done all he could. My mother told me that she had extracted a confession from my father that he had been foolishly lending Sylvestre money—in fact, that it was by helping Sylvestre financially, and tiding him over a "temporary" crisis, that he had been able to obtain his help. It had all come to nothing, and Sylvestre was bankrupt, so it was as if my father had thrown the money into the sea. This was bad news indeed, and my mother talked a little wildly about going out and earning her own living in some way.

The sight of my paintings cheered them a little,

98

and I found their pride pathetic, for they seemed to think I had only to show them in order to spring into fame and prominence.

"You exhibit them in New York," my father said. "People will buy them fast enough there. You've got friends in New York who'll fall over themselves to get them."

"I don't want to sell my pictures to friends," I explained, though I knew how hopeless it was to try to explain anything to him. "Besides, I don't know what friends you imagine I have there. Certainly none that buy pictures."

"You've got lots of friends there," he said grandly, "and what's more I think it's high time we went back. We're none of us doing any good here. And I'm disappointed in Paris. It hasn't come up to my expectations this time."

This kind of talk very naturally incensed my mother.

"And how do you suppose we're to get back? And what should we do when we got there? How should we live?"

To these questions he would not even condescend to reply.

I soon saw that I should have to give up my classes. Monsieur Vacaire, kind old man though he was, would not be likely to let me go on studying for nothing, even if I would have agreed to do so, for he

99

was poor, and his wife an expensive invalid. This was almost more than I could bear, and I cried hopeless tears on Ella Steevens' thin shoulder. She made me borrow from her enough money to buy frames for my pictures, and she took them to an obscure dealer who was kind to the unknown—but there they remained.

I felt as though an iron chest were closing over me then, closing down, down, down, so that it was becoming more and more difficult for me to breathe. Wherever I turned I met a wall, however I moved I was cramped and stifled. Ella tried to comfort me by repeating that I was not meant for misery and obscurity, that better times were coming.

"Oh, Ella!" I would cry, "*when* are they coming, *when* are they coming?"

I used to look back on that week-end with Richard and David at Bolsover as a little glimpse into a heaven I would never see again. If it had not been for Richard's letters and Ella's comfort I should have despaired. I did not write to Richard about giving up my classes, for I knew how it would distress him.

Then I realized I had heard nothing from Edouard since my return, and wrote to him asking when I might see him. In a few days there came a "pneumatique" from him asking me to lunch on the day following, and saying he would meet me at the studio door. It was to be my last day there, and a miserable

100

day it was. I knew I could not paint at the apartment, the rooms were too small and dark, and it seemed to me that everything was over and that there was nothing else for me to do but to begin giving English lessons, or take any other job that I could find. But when I got outside and saw Edouard, my own troubles were momentarily forgotten.

In a few weeks Edouard had grown flabby, almost thin. His clothes hung loosely on his altered body, and he looked like a man who had been very near death. I suppose I showed my amazement and concern plainly enough, for he greeted me by saying harshly:

"Yes, it is certainly I, Edouard de Solieux. Don't be afraid to speak to me. Come along, we will go to lunch somewhere where we have never been before. It is a charming day, is it not?" (There was a cold rain, mixed with sleet.) "And how are you, my dear Marna? I can see that you are well and happy, too. We shall be a gay pair. So much the better."

He put me into a cab and we drove across the river. During that drive his eyes kept filling with tears, and then he would burst out laughing and sing snatches of songs, beating time with my hand.

"See how gay I am! People keep telling me I look ill or sad. Not at all! not at all, I was never happier. 'Maman, dîtes-moi ce cu'on sent quand on aime——'

What a charming world. No wonder we all clamour
to be born——"

"Edouard!" I exclaimed, "what in the world's the
matter?"

"Ah, you ask me that too. Matter? What should
be the matter? Is not God in his heaven? Somebody
has said so. Is not this the best of all possible
worlds? Undoubtedly it is. 'Auprès de ma
blonde——' " he sang loudly, using my hand as a
baton.

I might have thought him drunk if I had not *known*,
instinctively, that it was something very different that
ailed him. We arrived at a gilded-looking restaurant
that I had never seen before and were immediately
shown upstairs. Then I saw that the waiter was holding open a door for us and I was suddenly frightened.
I knew, vaguely, that in many of the Paris restaurants
there were private rooms, but I had never dreamed
of finding myself in one. I stood there like a school-
girl, completely taken by surprise, and showing it. I
looked at Edouard in amazement, feeling disconcerted and chilled.

"Edouard! Why—why are we coming here? I
don't like this."

He put an arm through mine, urging me forward.

"My dear Marna, am I suddenly a monster?
Haven't I good reasons, always, for the things I do?
Besides, do you wish to see me cry like a baby in pub-

lic? No? Very well, let me cry in private, I assure
you you will like it better."

I looked through the door which the waiter held
open and saw a small room or *loge* which seemed to
form part of a gallery above the restaurant, which
was oval in shape. One side of the room was open
so that one could see down into the restaurant below
and those below could also have seen up but for a
small curtain on a brass rod that ran across the front
of the box. A table was already spread with a white
cloth and decorated with flowers, and there were no
chairs, only a red velvet sofa which was drawn up beside the table. I knew there was no nonsense about
Edouard, that he had no idea of making love to me
and that if he wished to bring me to a private room
it was for quite other reasons. Also I was so depressed and unhappy myself that I did not very much
care. I sat down and took off my gloves and hat.

"Sensible girl. Now let us see what we shall eat.
I haven't ordered. Nowadays I live on ashes and
tears. However—I must think of you. We will have
an omelette, fines herbes, poussins, asparagus, sauce
mousseline, then a soufflée. There, I cannot think
any more about things to eat." When the waiter had
gone he sat down beside me, and suddenly he put
his head in my lap and cried: "Mama, I want to die,
I want to die!"

"Edouard!" I exclaimed, passing my hands over his hair, "what is it? Tell me."

"I have been burning in hell for days and days," he sobbed, his voice muffled by my dress, "I have been to the valley of death, but couldn't get in, I have prayed for oblivion, I have tried drugs, nothing keeps me from thinking, nothing stops the agony. Oh, Mama, I who love life, I want to die, to die!"

I could think of only one thing that could have caused him this awful misery. I asked in a low voice:

"Is *she* dead?"

He raised his head and wiped his eyes, unashamed as a child.

"Such good fortune as that was not for me."

He rested his head on his hands, elbows on the table, and made a mighty effort to control himself: I saw his face working, as though he were trying to bear pain almost beyond his endurance. Then he poured out the whole story in rapid, broken sentences. He told me what had happened to him in my absence with a satirical bitterness directed at himself, with irony at his own sufferings, and running through it all genuine, agonizing grief. His mistress, the woman he had adored for six years, had left him, disappeared, without a word of explanation or good-bye. Frantic with anxiety, fearing some disaster, he accidentally learned that she had gone away

104

with de Rambaud, his friend— "And when I knew
that, I did not wish to open my eyes on another day."
It seemed he had introduced them to each other at
some chance meeting like ours at a restaurant. De
Rambaud had at once succumbed to her beauty and
her charm——"So did all men. But that *she*——"
Oh, no, he could never have believed it. For six
years, he told me, they had adored each other, they
had never had a quarrel, never an angry word, never
a reproach or cause for reproach. "But I am fat and
de Rambaud is a handsome man. I am short, de
Rambaud is tall. I have dark hair growing thin, anyone can see that—and he has thick, fair hair. I am a
man who feels, who suffers, who loves—he is a fine
animal. Oh, Marna, if you are capable of suffering,
harden yourself, harden yourself before it is too late,
for you offer a target to the devil which he cannot
resist."

Then I told him I had seen them, for I saw no point
now in not telling him, and he looked more tortured
than ever and asked me a thousand questions as
though he wished to visualize them together exactly as
I had seen them. I shall never forget our strange
lunch that day in the private room, while people below us laughed and chattered and Edouard made me
eat the food he could not eat himself, and questioned
me and returned again and again to that accidental
meeting in the South. Was she not beautiful? Had

I ever seen a woman so lovely? That face, to break one's heart, those eyes, to see into the soul—and she had seen only de Rambaud's body.

"It is that that is killing me," he said. "She is brilliant, she has a clear, fine mind, penetrating, intellectual. A hundred times I have said to myself: 'It is very probable that she will one day meet a man who is cleverer than I am, who has a better understanding of life, who will teach her more, who will exercise more power over her imagination, and that man she will prefer to me, and I will say that it is right and proper that she should. I will bow to fate as bravely as I can.' But never, *never* did I dream that she would leave me without one word, and for a man who is a mere animal—for *that* man——Oh, no! Oh, no!"

Poor Edouard! Since my experience with Frank Bellamy I had never seen a man suffer so, and as this man was not suffering for me I could all the better sympathize with his grief. I felt young, inexperienced and rather lost as I tried to comfort him. I knew nothing of the woman, nor of what she might have been expected to do, but I guessed that she was merely tired of Edouard and did not wish to face his misery. I guessed also that the fact that a woman is well developed mentally does not necessarily prevent her from falling wholly physically in love, though I felt very certain I could never do so myself.

He told me he thought of fighting a duel with de
Rambaud, of going to Italy for that purpose and
either killing him or being killed, but his English
blood forced him to see the ridiculous and futile side
of this performance, so he was pulled both ways. He
longed to kill his rival, and at the same time he saw
a comic picture of a fat man drawing a revolver. He
was only a silly, fat man anyway, he said, and that,
doubtless, was how the world regarded him. But
at last he was calmer, he had told someone, and felt
better. He had left his home, as he could not bear
his agony to be witnessed by his too adoring parents,
and was at a hotel, whither a confidential servant forwarded his letters. Presently he asked me about myself, and when I told him all my news he looked at
me with sad brown eyes that no longer sparkled, and
said:

"At any rate, God loves us very much, as he is chas-
tening us with such thoroughness and such an exquisite art. Well, we will try to comfort one another."

Then he fell into a deep silence and did not speak
at all, and I sat thinking about our lives, and telling
myself that I would rather have Edouard's troubles
than my own.

Suddenly he got up and said:

"Come, we must go. What was I thinking of to
bring you here? What selfish beasts men are!
Wounded by one woman we turn and bite the hand of

another. Forgive me for having been so stupid, so thoughtless. My dear Marna, please say you will. I think I was mad. I know I was mad."

"Does it matter very much?" I said. "Who is there to know? You were in trouble, and I was too miserable myself to care about anything very much."

"I make a poor return for your goodness," he said. "Forgive me."

He hurried me out, we got into a cab and drove home. He did not come in, but sent polite messages to my mother, and begged me to forget how far he had forgotten himself that day. He was so thoroughly distressed about it that I told him not to be foolish, that I would never think about it again. He made me a formal and respectful adieu, and did not even kiss my hands. His changed behaviour puzzled me a little, but he was so unhappy that I supposed he hardly knew what he was doing or saying.

Not many days later, I think it was less than a week, an astonishing thing happened.

I paid a hurried visit to the art dealer one afternoon to see if he had disposed of any of my pictures. (He had not, but he held out hopes.) I got back to the apartment about four o'clock, and to my surprise heard women's voices in the drawing-room—a hideous little room filled with the most appalling pieces of furniture I ever saw—and stood outside for a moment wondering who it could be. Then to my sur-

prise I recognized the cold, harsh voice of Madame
de Solieux in conversation with my mother. If the
wife of the French President had come to call I would
not have been more amazed. I went in and saw the
two sitting bolt upright, facing one another, in little
stiff gilt chairs, and the sight moved me to inward
mirth. I said good-afternoon to Madame de Solieux
and saw a look of supreme thankfulness on my mother's face.

"Marna," she said, "Madame de Solieux"—she
stumbled over the name, as she was never sure of
French words—"has come to ask——"

"Pardon, madame," Madame de Solieux broke in.
"May I speak?" She used her own language with
formal correctness as if it were a foreign tongue.
Edouard had told me she avoided Americans, and
the only English people she ever spoke to were members of her own immediate family. "May I explain,
mademoiselle? I have already placed the matter before your mother, and as you are not a child, no doubt
you would wish to hear what I have come to say, and
in my own words. My beloved son, Edouard"—she
paused for a moment as though she were gathering
all her self-control, all her forces—"my beloved son,
Edouard, has lately informed me that he wishes to
marry. For some time I myself have felt he would
be happier married, and I had selected, in my own
mind, several charming and suitable young girls, the

109

daughters of my friends, as possibilities. But it
seems that he has already made a choice." (What
family scenes and remonstrances, I wondered, lay
behind all this?) "It seems that his affections are
already involved, and as I have only my son's happiness at heart, I"—again she hesitated, like a horse
gathering energy for a leap—"I have been prevailed
upon to approach you and your mother and ascer-
tain your feelings in this matter. For naturally you
understand, mademoiselle, that it is you whom my
son wishes to marry."

Oh, what it must have cost her to say this! I was
not too astonished to guess what she was going
through. Totally unexpected and surprising though
this thing was, I knew it had something to do with
Edouard's unhappiness, and an appreciation of my
extremely precarious position in life. Perhaps there
was still more in it than that, but I could not think it
out then and there. My chief desire was to put an
end to this farcical and almost unbearable interview.
On my mother's face was an abashed, bewildered, almost bruised look, and I could guess what she had
suffered at Madame de Solieux's hands. As for the
latter, the fact that she had nerved herself, forced herself to do a thing she loathed and hated was plainly
visible in her harsh, strong-featured face.

I had not sat down. I could not bring myself to
draw up another of those little stiff chairs, so I re-

mained standing, wondering what I could say to
Madame de Solieux that would sound neither rude
nor awkward. At last I said.

"Thank you, Madame de Solieux, for telling me
this. I had no idea at all that Edouard thought of
marrying me, although we're such very good friends."
(A tremor of disgust passed over her face.) "I appreciate it more than I can say, but I would like to
talk it over with my mother first, and think about it.
I'm very much surprised. I never dreamt——"

She rose to her feet.

"Very well, mademoiselle. Then there is nothing
further that need be said at present. I repeat, I wish
only my son's happiness——"

"Well, Mama's happiness matters a little, too," my
mother broke in. She felt braver, now that I was
there. "It does to us, anyway."

Madame de Solieux looked at her rather as the
Palace of Versailles might look at a modern four-
roomed villa.

"Naturally, madame." She bowed her head and
moved toward the door, which I hastened to open for
her. On our way to the front door, which was down
a little dark hall, we were almost overpowered by the
smell of onions. Our servant, Jeanne, had just come
in and was preparing a savoury stew for dinner, for
even the poor must eat. Never before or since have
I been made to feel so acutely the meanness and the

111

vulgarity of poverty. There it was—a black little hall, the smell of onions, and myself in shabby coat and hat, letting out this grande dame. (My mother had let her in, wearing an apron, as she had been washing out some underclothes.) There was no sign of taste or grace anywhere, only a genteel squalor that sickened me. How she loathed it, that woman, and how she made me loathe it. If there are other incarnations, I am wicked enough to hope that Madame de Solieux will be obliged to spend at least one as the wife of an unsuccessful pedlar of shoelaces.

When I went back to my mother I found her crying. The experience had been too much for her. I tried to comfort her by telling her that there was a little surprise in store for our recent guest, as I had no intention whatever of marrying Edouard. But I could not stop her crying, and she became hysterical and sobbed and talked wildly. We were miserable, miserable people, better dead. It was awful to go on living like this. We lived in a mean, hideous place that sickened a woman like Madame de Solieux to come into, and we could not even pay the rent. We would have to get out, and soon, God only knew where we would go—to the workhouse, probably, if there were such things in France. She said she hated my father, she wished she had died before she had ever seen him; he had only brought misery on us. She hated him, hated, hated, hated him. I gave her am-

monia and quieted her at last, but even then she kept
crying out:

"You'd better marry that man. There's no other
hope for you or for any of us. You'd better marry
him. At least you won't have to live like a pig."

When my father came home that night—he was
invariably out all day, seeing people, tramping
about the streets, trying to borrow money, I now suspected—he looked terribly tired and his face was
grey. For the first time in my life I saw that he
looked discouraged. My mother would not see him
or speak to him, but stayed in bed and refused any
dinner. I said nothing to him about the day's happenings, and he sat reading the Paris *Herald*, and
sighing heavily.

"Oh, God!" I thought, "how am I to get out of
this, and get them out?"

I wrote to Madame de Solieux myself that night,
and said that it was quite impossible for me to marry
Edouard, as I did not love him. (I could imagine
how her face looked when she read this.) I wrote to
Edouard at the same time, and asked him why he had
not spoken to me about it, and saved his mother all
that anxiety. After all, he was only half French, and
I was not French at all. I also asked him to take me
to lunch soon, and we could then discuss it quietly.

When he did I understood everything. He had had
four different motives for acting as he did. Motive

113

one, he was desperately sorry for me as well as fond of me, and really thought he might make me happy; motive two, he wanted to put a stop to his mother's matrimonial schemes on his behalf; motive three, he hoped that in that way he might change his thoughts and ease his own sufferings; motive four, he was bitterly ashamed of himself for having taken me, a young unmarried woman, and one whom he respected deeply, to a private room, and wished to make amends.

I do not know whether he was relieved or not when he found me obdurate. I think he really believed we might have been happy together. But even if I had loved him, the thought of living his life and having Madame de Solieux for a mother-in-law would have kept me from marrying him. And I knew that I was a complex creature, full of entities most of which would have remained unsatisfied, and when I put the matter before them all in solemn council, with one accord they shouted, "No!"

CHAPTER VI

HEN came a time of misery and disaster. The art school saw me no more. We sent Jeanne away and did our own cooking, and I looked about me for some sort of employment. In Paris this was not easy to find, for I knew no one, but Edouard set to work and sought out several people who wished to take English lessons, and in intervals between cooking, sewing and housework—all of which I disliked—I went by bus and underground to their homes to teach. I had no idea how to begin, I had no system and no knowledge of the subject, but somehow I got on well enough, and made friends with the third wife of an elderly lecturer at the Sorbonne. This lady was young and pretty and very frivolous, and we had some amusing times together. She had married for security and a home, and, having only a small *dot,* her choice had not been large. I asked myself why I could not have done the same. What was there in me, I wondered, that kept me from acting prudently and with a view to my own worldly good? But the very thought of it seemed to rouse a fighting animal in me, a kind of clawing wild-cat of independence, and I knew I could never secure a place in life by a prudent marriage. It seemed natural enough that other people should do so, but I was different, and for me it was unthinkable.

I well remember the first time my father asked me for money. With a little cough, jingling some keys in his pocket, he told me he was going to get all the money he needed next week from a French financier who believed in his inventions past and future and was ready to put up hundreds of thousands of francs to get them on the market. He had discussed with him a new process he had in mind for making briquettes, and the financier was definitely interested. But at present he was somewhat pressed for cash. Could I spare a little? I could. I had been paid by Madame Rouget that morning. I handed the money over to him.

"But father, haven't we any money left at all?"

He tried to hide a look of distress.

"Well, just at this moment, no. But next week my man will put up whatever I want him to. Then we'll be all right. I'm sorry to have to borrow from you, but it will only be for a day or two."

Clearly we could not go on like that. Money had to be found for the housekeeping, for rent, for my father's expenses, for my own—my poor mother stayed at home—and my earnings at present only covered a quarter of this. About this time a cheerful letter came from Richard. He had been staying with the R——s in Durham—delightful people whom I would like. He and his brother were taking a moor in Scotland for the grouse season. He wished I could come. There was a good deal of anxiety about Ireland. What did I think of the latest exploits of the suffragettes? How was I getting on with my work? He hoped I was painting hard and selling pictures.

Why, oh why, I wondered, did this world in which Richard lived exist so gaily, while I had only misery, stress, anxiety and boredom? It was not fair, it was not fair! I locked myself in my room with his letter and gave way to despondent tears. I saw nothing but dullness and misery ahead of me. I was young. Given opportunities, I might have made something of myself, but everything was snatched away from me before I could grasp it. In that moment I seemed to touch the very bottom of my unhappiness and, having touched it, I began to survey my prospects from a new angle. I was evidently not meant to live easily, as so many others lived; I belonged instead to the world that struggles and suffers, and I might as well make up my mind to it. That life does not come up to our expectations is the chief source of our misery, and therefore I would expect nothing, nothing. What had led me to anticipate an agreeable life? My parents' hopes for me, their talk, ever since I could remember anything, of the good

117

things to come when we should be rich, of my right
to happiness, all this now seemed to me empty and
mischievous. I determined to put it behind me for
ever, and live arduously, expecting nothing. Richard
was a false note in my life; he threw it out of key;
he was a high light that dimmed all the rest. In a
mood of bitter renunciation that made me take a
delight in cruelty—a double cruelty, as it wounded
myself first—I wrote him a letter, and tried to keep
the tears from falling on the paper. I told him that
his life and mine were worlds apart, that moors in
Scotland and the activities of suffragettes were
equally unimportant to me, that my friends were
plain people who had hard lives like my own, and
that the sooner I went out of his life the better. I
took a fierce joy in what I was saying, and posted
the letter without a regret. That was over. I had
smoothed out the inequalities of my existence. I saw
now where I stood and what I was. I cooked the
dinner that night and pictured myself as cooking dinners and worrying about the next day's food till the
end of my life. As for my father and mother, I
realized that they looked upon me as their guide and
helper, and that I must never leave them.

One day in April my father came home and sat
quietly in a chair without moving or speaking. His
face was grey and expressionless, as though his mind
were emptied of all thought. He sat through dinner

118

in almost complete silence, and ate little. When my mother implored him to tell her what was the matter he said he was all right. When she asked, "Is it about money?" he answered that it was not that, for he had been promised all the money he needed next week. (It was always next week.) But after I had gone to bed my mother came into my room, looking white and frightened.

"Your father is very ill," she said. "He's been to see a doctor—several doctors, he says—and they all tell him the same thing. He has to have an operation. If he doesn't have it he may just drop dead." She collapsed into a chair. "Oh, Mama, what are we going to do? What are we going to do?"

I became very matter-of-fact, as was my habit in a crisis of this sort.

"Do? Why he must have the operation, of course. What else is there to do? When do they want him to have it?"

"Soon—just as soon as possible. They seem to think there's great danger. Oh, your poor father!"

She began to cry, hopelessly.

"Now, mother, people have had operations before, and survived them. Don't be foolish. I expect he can go into a hospital and be very well looked after. I'll ask Edouard about it."

"But we've no money. You know we haven't. How are we going to pay for anything? How are

119

we going to live? Oh, it's awful, it's awful——!"

"If he's got to have an operation he's got to have it, that's all, money or no money. Doctors aren't devils. It's their business to save life. They'll wait. Now don't worry about that. Tell him I'll look after everything. We'll manage. You'd better go and see the doctor with him yourself to-morrow."

Presently she went back to her room somewhat re-assured by my optimistic tone, and for a long time I lay with my face to the wall, picturing God as a kind of Torquemada, inventing new tortures.

"Go on, go on," I thought. "I don't care what you do. Think of all the frightful things you can, I don't care. What does anything matter? Soon I'll be dead, we'll all be dead, and we won't remember anything. Nothing you can do really matters, because we can always die and forget it."

During my father's operation and for some weeks after his death I kept no diaries, and so hideous was that time, so deplorable, that I have no wish to recall it. I remember in a confused, nightmarish way, the bearded, squat little doctor, who seemed to me clever but ghoulish. I think nothing could have saved my father's life. So suddenly did this illness come upon him that he had little time for anxiety or despair, and only at the end did he seem to realize the situation in which he was leaving us. So I lied to him, I told him lie after lie. I said my pictures were all sold (one was sold), and that the dealers were clamouring for more; that Ella Steevens and I had a scheme for opening an Anglo-American tea-shop, and that Ella was going to put up the money. (She had sometimes talked of it.) He always had a sweet expression, and was considered a rather handsome man, but his look was now so gentle and peaceful that I knew he was going to die—the doctors held out little hope—and that he was dying in the confident belief that we should be able to get on all right without him. Faults he had, but they were only improvident, unbusiness-like faults, and as a husband and father he had been absolutely unfailing in his devotion and love. He had thought only of us. His unpractical hopes and vague, over-ambitious dreams had been only for us.

I had to borrow enough money from Edouard to pay all expenses, including rent and doctor's bills, and the cost of the funeral. He knew well enough how slight were the chances of my being able to pay it back for a very long time, but he lent it willingly and simply, and without any exaggerated gestures. Soon afterwards we left Paris, two sad women in dyed black, with debts in front of us and tragedy be-hind.

The Lawtons, hearing of my father's death, had at once written and asked us to stay with them. This my mother longed to do, so I thanked them for their goodness and accepted. There was really nowhere

121

else for us to go until I could look about me and find some way of making money. So to Putney we went and were solemnly received. There was a great deal of talk of the comforts of religion and the mysterious ways of the Lord, which, though I tried not to let it, jarred on me unbearably, but to my harassed mother it was heaven there. For once she was relieved of all care and worry, for once she felt her feet on solid ground—and oh, how solid it was!—for once she felt secure and at peace. She and Celia got on very well, and I felt Celia would have made a far more satisfactory daughter for her than I did. Mr. Lawton suggested various kinds of employment for me, but I wanted to find something for myself, for which I need not be indebted to him. I had heard nothing, of course, from Richard, nor did I expect ever to see him again. The pain of this separation and my loss gave me a sort of bitter pleasure and was a counter-irritant, but at the same time my heart stood still when I saw someone who resembled him, or read his or his brother's name in the papers.

One day I saw a review of a first novel and it set me thinking. It was by a young girl who had never been out of England, and it was a simple chronicle of a girl's life for two years after leaving school. The reviewer spoke highly of it and predicted for the young author a brilliant future—which prediction has not, I may say, been fulfilled. But I suffered a

122

sharp spasm of jealousy. Here was an inexperienced girl of twenty embarking on a promising literary career. Why not I, who had suffered and experienced so much? What had she that I had not? Why had my letters always been easy and pleasant to write, and why had Richard said that I wrote the best letters he had ever received? Didn't that point to at least a slight literary talent? At any rate, I made up my mind to try.

I wrote an article on the life of a girl art student in Paris, and sent it to one of the women's magazines. It was returned to me, but I tried another and another, and the third took it and paid me three and a half guineas. (It was a long time before I learnt to translate guineas and half guineas into pounds, shillings and pence with any ease!) I had paid six shillings to have it typed, and the profit seemed to me enormous. If I could do only one such article a week I could live. I was thrilled by the discovery of a new and lucrative talent.

"But Marna, I always said you could write if you tried," my mother said. She had, but I pointed out to her that in that way she .closely resembled nearly all other mothers.

It was difficult to write at the Lawtons'. I could not very well demand a room to myself where I could work in peace, and I was obliged to share a large double-bedroom with my mother, which seemed to me

humiliating and cramping. As soon as I had had
two articles accepted I made up my mind that I would
find a room in London and live by myself, and I did
so. This was, I think, the most daring step I ever
took, but I took it, leaving my mother in Putney,
where she was quite content to be.

I wrote to Edouard, to tell him my news, and gave
him my address. He wrote back that he was not at
all surprised; that a talent for writing very often accompanied a talent for painting, and he believed I
would do well.

My room was in a street near Oxford Street, at the
back of Selfridge's. I wrote frenziedly all day, and
often till bedtime. I made great friends with my
landlady, who was quite willing that my week's pay-
ments should sometimes be delayed, and she promised not to worry me. I saw no one. I was shabby
and morbidly aware of it, and took my walks about
London as unseen as a wandering ghost, and two
evenings a week went to Putney to dine.

It was once again "the season," and it seemed to
me supremely silly that in a world of cruelty and
uncertainty, a world of despair and disappointment,
people should take so seriously the business of amusing themselves. Did they not know they had to die?
Did they not know that under their expensive skins
were skeletons? Did they not know that every one
of the questions man asked about the universe re-

mained unanswered? So deeply did these feelings go in me that I have never been able to eradicate them. All sorts of "complexes" that trouble me now were set up by those days of loneliness, a loneliness that promised to be unending. No one ever recovers from a really unhappy youth. It leaves ineffaceable marks.

One afternoon I came home at about five from a walk in Regent's Park and was told by Mrs. Smythson that a gentleman had called to see me and, finding me out, had said he would be back within an hour.

"What sort of a gentleman?" I asked, my heart beating wildly.

She said he was tall, and then she used that pleasant old word, nearly obsolete now, "Quality."

"I thought," she added, "as Mr. Whitty is out, miss, you might like to use his sitting-room."

I said I would, and thanked her, and hurried up to tidy myself. I suddenly realized how crazily I had acted, how cruelly and stupidly. Suppose Richard did not come back, so that I should never be able to tell him so? Suppose he changed his mind? I sat in Mr. Whitty's sitting-room on the ground floor in a fever of anxiety. It was the sort of room that will continue to be seen in London lodgings, I suppose, for years to come. There were the usual green things in pots, the usual crochet tidies on the chairs and the usual Marcus Stones on the walls. There were no books or papers, or any hint, anywhere, of a mind or character in Mr. Whitty—a man of forty or so I had sometimes seen in the hall—but only a suggestion of a meagre body that sat on chairs and fed itself and moved in and out of the door.

Then a car stopped outside and Richard rang the pealing bell. I ran to let him in.

He kissed my cheek, but we didn't speak till we were sitting side by side on the sofa. Then he said:

"What a silly! What a silly! Why did you do it?"

But I saw that he understood, and that he had forgiven me.

He told me my letter had hurt him terribly, for he had at once—(did I not know that unfortunate nature of his yet?)—jumped to the conclusion that I no longer cared about him, that I had fallen in love, that I had changed. He was old, I was young, he was married and could do nothing for me, I was already tired of a friendship that "led nowhere." He did not dream, then, that my letter was inspired by disappointment and pain, until he saw Edouard and heard what had happened. I told him everything, treating him like a confessor, and the relief this gave me was indescribable. He insisted on knowing exactly how much I had borrowed from Edouard, for he intended repaying it, preferring that I should look to him for help. And then we once more talked seriously of money. He was a rich man, I was poor, he had friends, position, a secure and interesting life, I had nothing but my youth, and that must not be spent in anxiety.

"You know me well enough now, Marna, to understand how I feel about money. If it is useless as a means of helping others, the possession of it is a pretty poor thing. You *must* let me help you. No absurd prejudices must stand in the way. More silliness has been talked about money than about any other subject. A man mustn't help a woman because if he does he is supposed to want something in return; he is popularly supposed to be trying to buy her. It's vile, and worse, it's untrue; certainly where you and I are concerned. Now I am going to pay Edouard, and I am going to make you a small present whenever you need it, and let there be no nonsense about it. As for your attempting to repay it, that is out of the question, and I won't hear of it now or ever. I give, and it gives me pleasure to give."

I told him my life was nothing without him, that I was unutterably grateful, that I was bitterly ashamed of my letter, and that we must never have another misunderstanding—though for those we had had I was ready to take the blame.

"There's only one thing I want now," I told him, "and that is a typewriter. If you'll let me have that——"

He looked at his watch. It was too late to go out and buy it now, but he would call for me at ten, and we would go out and buy one then, and anything else I needed. He kissed me good-bye with all his old gentleness and tenderness, and I ran up to my room, feeling more light-hearted than I had felt for many months. Life with Richard in it was a life I could contemplate with hope, even confidence. I felt that the worst of my sorrows were behind me, and I went to bed early, so that the morning would come all the sooner.

My literary career began with the purchase of a Corona. With a singleness of mind unhampered by friends, family, social engagements or outside interests, I wrote articles and short stories and sent them, in impressive numbers, to magazines and periodicals. Richard, when he learned of my few successes and many failures, advised an agent, and sent me to a Mr. Lenyard, a pleasant, shrewd, capable person, better liked by authors than publishers, and the very man, therefore, that I needed. He did so much better for me than I could do for myself that I did not begrudge him the ten per cent which was his right.

Richard was obliged to be away a great deal, and then I saw no one. He wanted to find friends for me, but I was in no mood to make the necessary effort and begged him not to bother. He had spoken to

me more than once about a man named Morisan, who
edited a literary monthly, and whom he thought I
should like, and one day I was surprised to receive a
letter from Mrs. Morisan asking me to lunch. She
said it was not a party, she quite understood that I
was in mourning, and she hoped very much that I
would come. I wrote and told her I should be delighted, and rather fearfully I went.

They lived in a pleasant house in Connaught
Square, and it seemed to me that day the very acme of
everything that was comfortable and in good taste.
There were only Mrs. Morisan herself and her niece, a
quiet, unremarkable girl who was up from the country
for a few days. Mrs. Morisan was a new type to
me, and interested me so much that I forgot myself
entirely. She was dark, witch-like, angular, and not
young—she must have been nearly fifty—and at no
time could she have been physically attractive, but
there was something intense and compelling about
her, perhaps due to the way she thrust her head forward upon her long, too slender neck, and looked
closely into the face of the person she was speaking
to. She talked a good deal about fortune-telling—
she begged me to go to a Mrs. Pauncefort-Thrale, and
wrote down her name and address—and about spiritualism, and told me she was very psychic. A good
deal of her talk I thought extravagant and absurd,
but I was perfectly prepared to like her in spite of

it. She was not interested in books except those dealing in mysticism and Eastern lore, and she kept incense burning before a little Buddha in a small shrine in a corner of the drawing-room. She said I must meet some of her husband's literary friends, and suggested a night for dinner the following week, and I went away, pleased with my visit.

The instant I saw Mrs. Morisan again I felt at once that she was no longer interested in me. She was aloof and off-hand, though never, of course, impolite. She introduced me to her husband, and had I been older and more worldly I would have understood her behaviour, for I saw that he was years younger than she was, and a very attractive man indeed. It was a rainy night, I had gone there by bus, I was feeling shy and alone, and very far from confident or cheerful. After his wife's coolness, Mr. Morisan's cordiality and friendliness was like balm to me, and he made me feel something more than a shabby nobody. I felt that she regretted having asked me, and this was true enough, as I afterwards learned. She was an unhappy creature, for whom, had I known all the circumstances, I should have been very sorry. A rich woman, she had married an exceedingly attractive man much younger than herself and lived in a perpetual fever of anxiety lest he should fall in love with someone. Into this dangerous domestic atmosphere I was suddenly plunged, thinking only of

130

myself and of my own difficulties, and entirely unconscious that troubles of another sort were charging
the air all around me.

I made myself as agreeable as I could to both of
them, and with entire innocence, and listened not
without awe to the highly intelligent conversation of
a Mr. and Mrs. Greythorne, both swells in the literary
world. When the evening was over the Greythornes
departed on foot, as they lived almost next door, and
when someone suggested a taxi for me I said I was
going home by bus. This Mr. Morisan said was
ridiculous, and he sent for a cab, at which I was much
embarrassed, as I had almost no money. When it
came, however, he put me in and got in himself.
I could see that his wife thought this quite unnecessary, and was displeased, but he had evidently
guessed at the state of affairs, and on the way, said:

"Do you mean to say you go out at night with
only a few pennies in your purse?"

"Yes. Not that I do go out very often. This is
the first time I've been invited out to dinner in a
private house since I've been in London."

He asked me where I had met Richard, and I told
him.

"He's your great admirer, and he thinks you have
a future. What are you writing now? Stories?
Articles?"

"Just now I'm trying to write short stories. Sometimes they come off, but I don't think I've quite got the hang of it yet. I will, though."

"Why don't you write a novel?"

"I've thought of it. I started one, but I tore it up. I hate callow novels, and I think mine might be."

"I don't know. In most cases I agree with you. I think it's better not to publish a novel till you're over thirty, but you've been about the world a good deal, and you haven't had an easy, comfortable life, which is all to the good. It seems to me it might be worth trying."

"You're very encouraging. Perhaps I will try."

"I'll help you find a publisher if you do."

"How very kind of you!"

"It isn't kind of me at all. Why shouldn't I want to help you? And if you deliver the goods, as I think you may, helping you will be a very easy and pleasant matter indeed."

As he was about to leave me at my door, he said:

"Perhaps you'll come and lunch with me one day, and we'll talk about this again."

I told him I should love to, and as he was about to get into the cab again, he said:

"I'll drop you a line if I may. Good-night."

When I was in my bedroom I tried to recall his face—with a singular lack of success. I remembered thinking that it would be a good face to draw, being clear-cut and well modelled; it was an interesting face, and the eyes decidedly good, but I found I could not recreate it. His personality, however, was almost overpoweringly present, and I woke up once or twice in the night to find myself thinking about him. The next morning I bought the literary monthly of which he was editor, and read it through carefully, wondering if I would ever be fortunate enough to contribute anything to it, and a little awed by the authoritative tone of its writers.

So slight was my contact with the world at this time that the happenings recorded in the daily papers seemed to me misty and unreal. When, late in June, I read about the murder of the Austrian Archduke at Sarajevo it seemed to me as cruel and silly as the murder of a farm-girl in Lincolnshire, and no more and no less. But Richard was concerned, and there was a tension and an anxiety in the articles dealing with the affair.

Mrs. Morisan evidently felt she had done her duty by me, and now lost interest in me. She doubtless had other reasons for not inviting me to her house again, but I knew nothing of them and suspected nothing. I was hurt by her unfriendliness. I had thought her odd, but likeable, and I had hoped that in her house, among her friends, my poverty and lack of background might not matter. I told myself that it was the sort of thing I must learn to expect from

women, and was glad when, on lunching with Mr.
Morisan, I found that we were to be alone.

Alan Morisan was in the unhappy position of a
man who feels he ought to be grateful to his wife for
her money and her help, and at the same time finds it
almost impossible to go on living with her. When
they had first met he was young and somewhat discouraged by reverses, but he soon discovered that
he could very well make his own way in the world,
and regretted his weakness with a bitterness that
time did nothing to lessen. I have often wondered
how much a man need be grateful to a woman for
having bought him in a moment of folly or discour-
agement, for her motives, when examined, are often
neither generous nor disinterested. Not till considerably later did I discover all this. Perhaps I
should have refused to see him when I perceived
how events were shaping, but I wonder how many
in my position would have done so. I had little
fondness for women. They seemed to me to be my
potential enemies, and Ella Steevens and my mother
were the only ones for whom I had any great affection. A woman friend would have made all the
difference to me in those days, but there was no such
person, so I turned to men for companionship all
the more readily.

I lunched with Alan Morisan not once but many
times. He had a caustic, sophisticated, rather bitter

mind, but he loved truth and constantly sought it.
He told me I was the first woman he had ever known
who had any liking for the abstract; who did not
seize upon the general, like a spider on a fly, and drag
it down to the particular after tearing off its wings.
I learnt that though he could not get on without
women's society he hated the power they had over
his senses, for he knew that in the long run they
would always bore him. So, I suspected, would I,
but I kept that suspicion to myself.

He soon contrived to see me daily. It became a
regular thing for us to lunch together, and once in a
while I had the joy of dining with him, usually in
some small restaurant in Soho. I may have been
acting foolishly and wrongly, but my loneliness had
driven me almost crazy for just such companionship;
I was like a man being hauled into a boat from a
black and icy sea.

Suddenly Richard had to go to America, and came
to say good-bye to me before he sailed. He promised
it would not be for more than a month, but it was
imperative that he should go. He was very anxious
about affairs in Europe, and I think hated to leave
just then, though he still had hopes that Austria would
be reasonable about the Sarajevo business. I told
him I was seeing a good deal of Alan Morisan, and
he said he thought I would find him an interesting
man and helpful to me. I hated to see Richard

go, for though he was extremely busy and I saw little of him, it was a great comfort to me merely to know that he was near at hand.

Alan took a less optimistic view than Richard of the situation in the Balkans.

"One or two more or less civilized nations," he said, "have about as much chance of keeping out of trouble in this world as a few sound people have of keeping their health in the midst of a cholera epidemic."

"Surely a real war is almost impossible nowadays," I protested.

"Every so often," he said, "the world goes mad. If it goes mad now, heaven help us."

He had little faith in the leaders anywhere except a few at home, who, he said were sane and sensible men. "But there'll be such a din that nobody'll listen to them."

We were together at the corner of Bond Street and Piccadilly one day when we saw placards announcing Austria's declaration of war on Serbia. That was on the 28th of July, and, if my diary tells the truth, a warm, bright day. Even then it seemed to me not to matter very much if two rather far away countries chose to make war on each other, but Alan knew better.

He exclaimed, "Good God!" and for some time we walked in silence, while I watched his grave face with apprehension. At last he said, "It will draw in Russia, Germany, France, and probably Italy. How on earth can we keep out of it? There isn't a hope. The insanity will soon be on us all. A really sensible man would undoubtedly shoot himself now and spare himself the bother and the boredom and the agony to come, but I suppose very few of us will be as sensible as that. Marna, human beings are so incredibly silly that it's pointless to go on reproducing them."

I could see that he was deeply shaken, and we went to a hotel while he had a drink and we talked about the idiocy of men setting out to kill each other violently and in great numbers when life, anyway, was so precarious and sad and difficult, and such an insoluble mystery. We were yet more appalled when the Germans burst through Luxembourg and began to overrun Belgium, and England declared war on Germany.

I suffered another sort of despair then, less personal, worse than anything I had yet known. Nothing was secure, nothing certain. The world was like a black and quaking bog into which human beings by the hundred thousand were soon to be swallowed up. War had always seemed to me the last horror, the Grand Guignol of the universe. I remembered books and stories about the Civil War; I could remember the Boer War, and these things could only be thought about without anguish because they were behind us. And now, again! And worse than ever!

Alan had a vivid and apprehensive imagination, and he visualized the horrors to come with painful clearness. The words "glory" and "victory" drove him almost frantic, and all the big empty words and silly, hollow phrases used at that time. We took a taxi after dinner on that August night and joined the crowds in front of Buckingham Palace. The King, we were told, had just said a few words, and the crowds still waited, pressing about the fountain and the gates, shouting, crying out, singing, while groups joined arms and surged and pushed and swayed this way and that.

"One will have to go to the war," said Alan, characteristically, "in order to get away from the people at home."

In front of the palace, glowing with incandescent brilliance under the arc-lights, were great beds of red geraniums, and to both of us they seemed to shout, "Blood! Blood!" It was an unforgettable scene and aroused unbearable emotions. We drove away and went into the park, where we sat down under the trees in the cool dusk. Alan drew me close to him and I laid my head on his shoulder. We were both tired out, physically and emotionally emptied, and for a long time we neither moved nor spoke. There were other couples under the dark trees, and they

138

seemed to me wise and right to go on making love while they could before they too were caught into the whirlpool.

"I've seen this coming for years," said Alan, and I knew he was not speaking of the war. "I've been attracted to a good many women in one way and another, but I've always known very definitely that I didn't want to spend my life with them. Now I've found someone I do want to spend my life with —though I never hoped to live after sixty, and don't now—so perhaps it's just as well that a lunatic in Serbia has shot an Archduke and killed him, because I see no very clear way out of this."

It was the first time he had spoken of his feelings toward me, and though I guessed them I had pretended to ignore them. I tried to raise my head, but he pressed it down on his shoulder again, and I remained as I was. I thought of Frank Bellamy, of Richard, of Alan himself and of others, and said with some bitterness:

"I seem to be the kind of woman men wish they had married."

He made no reply to this. He was thinking, trying to see his way.

"I'll have to go to this war. I'll go loathing and dreading it. I'll be uncomfortable, bored, frightened, disgusted, but I'll go. If and when I come back, I'll try to get Edith to divorce me. She'd be happier without me in the long run. She's like a woman who's been told she's going to be killed in an accident, and she's constantly wondering if the moment has come. She spends her time at fortune-tellers because she wants to find out if I'm unfaithful to her, or going to be, and with whom. I'm extremely sorry for her, but I can't make her happy. You're the type of woman I was bound to fall in love with. I'm not going to ask you any questions now. I know you're happy with me, as I am with you. And the future's too dark, too appallingly uncertain. I'm so exhausted I don't even want to kiss you. We'll sit here quietly a little longer, and then I'll take you home."

I made no answer, and was glad that there was no need for it. I thought it probable enough that I did or could love him. We had seemed familiar to one another from the first, and I had a kind of confidence in him; confidence in his mind and his judgments, and in his general rightness. The idea of divorce frightened me a little, for I had had no experience with it, nor had I known anyone who had been divorced, so that it seemed a thing to be avoided if possible. And at present it was all distant and extremely vague and problematical. For between us was the awful cloud of war.

He took me home, still unkissed, but mentally and spiritually I felt he was very close to me. He said

140

that he would see me soon. I knew that in his own
mind he no longer belonged to himself, that loyalty
had already chained him hand and foot to the monster
he dreaded and loathed. I think no one who went
to the war was braver than Alan Morisan, for he
feared and hated it from the bottom of his soul. I
think no one who made the sacrifice made it more
finely, for he never believed in it.

I no longer wanted to write, for there seemed
nothing worth writing about, nothing that the war
had not made to seem irrelevant and silly. I had
begun an article on "The Intelligence of Cats"—Ella
Steevens had a most remarkable cat, whose photo-
graphs I possessed—but in the morning I looked at
what I had written and tore it up. I wondered if I
could ever write again, and if I did not, how was I
going to live.

Alan joined the Artists' Rifles and began his training. The casualty lists had begun to come in, and
I read them in the morning papers with the tears
streaming from my eyes. Then, one day, I saw
David's name among the killed, and there was a kind
of inevitableness about its appearance. As I looked
at it, my mind flooded with memories, a strange
thing happened. The whole world seemed to me to
pause, to stand absolutely still, to hold its very breath,
and it was as if a little space in infinity had opened
before my eyes and I could look through. There

followed the most wonderful sensation I have ever
known. Sitting up in my bed in that drab room, holding the paper in my hands, I suddenly became aware
of complete *cessation*. There was no movement of
time, no noise, no action anywhere, no matter, but
only a profound and lovely consciousness of well-
being so acute as to be indescribable. It was as
though this exquisite sensation had come to me from
the brain of someone else—from David's brain; as
though for an eternal second his consciousness and
mine had occupied the same place in time and space;
as though they had mingled, so that what he felt, I
felt.

The emotions of that strange moment left me
shaken but curiously happy. It was all right.
Something lovely had happened to him, something
quite beyond my thick and dull imaginings. I longed
from the bottom of my soul to be able to keep
that exquisite sensation, to make it mine, but I knew
with sad certainty that it could not be kept. It
faded and was gone, leaving me only my inadequate
memories of it. And never, in all the years that
have passed since then, have I been able to recapture it.

At Putney Mrs. Lawton and Celia and my mother
rolled bandages. Mr. Lawton wrote letters to the
papers and tried to get himself accepted for some
sort of war work. I saw as much as I could of Alan.

However wrong it may have been—and was it?—
I know I made him as happy as it was possible for
him to be under such nightmarish conditions, and
kept him from extravagances and perils, and to me
he unburdened himself of all the thoughts and feelings
that piled themselves up in his excited brain. The
literary monthly was being edited now by his elder
brother. Alan commissioned me to write a series of
short articles on London in war time through a
woman's eyes, and found other work for me to do
which kept me from being entirely dependent on
Richard's generosity. I saw that there was little hope
of my being able to take my mother away from
Putney. The war would probably last, Alan said,
a year or eighteen months at least, and meanwhile
he thought it would be unwise to make any changes.

His training was intensive and severe. The more
he became absorbed into the great machine of war,
the less he stormed and protested and attacked. He
let himself be carried along by the current, and when
we met we talked of other things. Then the moment
came when the battalion was ordered to France, and
I begged him not to tell me when he went, and not
to come to say good-bye. But our resolutions were
swept away in the end, and one day I heard his knock
on my bedroom door as I sat writing. He was very
calm, and at first he talked quietly to me.

"I don't think I'm going to be killed," he said,

"because I don't care enough about living. It's the young enthusiast, the hot-blooded lover of life, the singer, the poet, who will be cut down. That's one of the many ironies of war. I'm tired and I don't give a damn, really, whether I live or die except for your sake, and whether I'll ever be anything but a thorn in your flesh is problematical. No, I don't mind dying, though now I know you I prefer to live. The things I'm afraid of are fear and pain and boredom, and those I'll get in full measure. But so will you, my poor darling, so will you!"

He spoke more truly than he knew.

It was a terrible parting for me. To this day I do not know whether I was in love with him or not. He filled my life, and perspective was lacking. He had sprung into my life, like some others, at a bound, and the times we lived in and my isolation had much to do with my fondness for him. Richard I certainly loved, with a steady and unwavering affection that will never alter, but the others who so strangely came and went absorbed me only for a time, and left me curiously free. I would have done anything for Alan then; his troubles were my troubles, his going was agony, and his influence on me deep and lasting, but his loss did not affect my capacity for loving again. Had I led a normal life, with friends and outside interests, I would not have given so much of myself nor been so deeply involved where I was in-

volved at all, but omni-present nature abhors a
vacuum, and except for those men and for my own
thoughts, my life was a vacuum indeed.

Our parting was painful, dreadful. His despair
at leaving me, his helplessness to control the situation to master his own fate or mine, made him almost
brutal, and his kisses had in them more of agony
for me than delight. When he had gone I had an
attack of the horrors, and threw myself on the bed,
wishing I might never rise from it. Human beings
seemed to me more pathetic and powerless than I
had ever dreamed they were, and the world more
cruel. And then for the first time I gradually became
aware of the sad consolation that comes from a sense
of fellowship in pain. I saw that none of us, no, not
one, could escape it. I had seen myself as a victim.
I now saw Man as The Victim, and his endurance
and fortitude wonderful beyond any words. And I
got up from the bed obscurely soothed and comforted.

CHAPTER VII

WAR, war, war! To live with war, to sleep, and dream of war, to have one's private life ruled by those who, from some lofty place in the government, regulate the behaviour of civilians during war, to be bombed, raided, to feel for ever insecure—to all these things men and women can and do grow accustomed. But what I, for one, could never grow accustomed to was that awful outpouring of blood across the Channel that went on and on, steadily, unceasingly, with no sign whatever of being staunched. Why this did not drive us all mad I do not know. I used to tell myself for the sake of my own sanity that a million deaths are really only one death, that a million human agonies are really one agony. Each one of those millions is capable of feeling only his own personal pain, agony multiplied to infinity can only be felt by each one in himself. War is only a man dying. War is only someone suffering. And men and women die and suffer every day. So I used to tell myself. The tragedy of a messenger boy run over by a bus in the Strand was the same tragedy that was being enacted and re-enacted thousands of times over in all the

146

theatres of war; the violence and pain were the same. When death comes to one, the war is over. One man, one death. These things I used to repeat to myself, and they helped me to endure what was unendurable.

My mother remained with the Lawtons, for they would not hear of my taking her away. I gave her what money I could for her small expenses, and lived on, economically enough, at Mrs. Smythson's. Richard had insisted on my taking the sitting-room downstairs once occupied by Mr. Whitty, and there I kept my books and papers, and could work in comfort. I wrote every morning, and from three in the afternoon until ten at night—except on Wednesday nights, when I had an evening off—I worked at a private nursing home for officers run by a Lady Brondish, a friend of Richard's. There I carried trays, answered the door, worked the lift, and did anything required of me. With my nurse's uniform I felt I put on another personality. I became less an agonized and ineffectual onlooker and more a tiny component of some vast organism, and so less subject to the erosion of thought and reason.

Richard returned from America at the end of August, 1914, and was absorbed at once by the Foreign Office. We saw each other when we could and exchanged letters when we could not. He looked older, thinner, as the war went on. He told me that most of his friends kept wondering why God had allowed the war to take place, and this made us both laugh. Why does God let a child die of burns? Why does God let the messenger boy be run over in the Strand? Why does God permit man to use his hands and brain for the perfecting of high explosives, and having allowed him to do so, was it likely that He would intervene to prevent his using them? Richard, however, was not a rebel like Alan, nor did he think with such hard clearness. He belonged to the class and generation that thought wars inevitable, and provided they were fought in a chivalrous and sportsmanlike manner, with a watchful eye on the Hague Convention, almost respectable. It seemed natural to him that there should be wars, and brave, unselfish fellows to go and fight them, but war waged by submarine and aircraft, by hospital-bombing and poison gas seemed to him sheer barbarism. He had been to the Boer War himself, and wished very much to go in some capacity to this one, but as yet saw no hope of it, and I prayed, meanwhile, that he would not. David's death—his only nephew, his brother's only son—had deeply saddened him, and I told him my strange experience in connection with it, hoping it would comfort him a little, and I think it did.

When Alan Morisan was killed at Bapaume in March, 1916, Richard was surprised at the grief I showed. I told him everything there had been between us, and he was torn by pity for Alan and at the same time by his old tormentor jealousy. When I could bear to talk about it at all we discussed, freely and frankly, my relation to him and to other men. I told him that I would undoubtedly marry some day, that he must expect it; also that I was certain to be attracted to men, and to grow fond of them, for it was my nature to do so. My affection for him was untouched and untouchable.

"I want above all things to see you happy," he said that day, "but I want your happiness to come through me. I think I even want your sorrows to come through me."

And yet he asked nothing from me but my devotion.

Alan wrote me a letter three days before his death. He was unusually cheerful, for him, and talked of leave. He asked me to send him at once Norman Douglas's *South Wind*, and the poems of A. E. Housman, which he wished to re-read. He wrote at the bottom of his letter, in a sort of humorous postscript,

"As for the war, I ignore it."

I had no such vision at the news of his death as I had had at David's. He was killed by a hidden sniper, leading his men in the attack on Bapaume. Later I learnt, from a wounded officer in his regiment, the very hour of his death. I was sitting at my table, writing quietly at the very instant that

Alan, who loved me, was going forward under shell fire to meet a violent death. Not a tremor disturbed the ether about me, not a vibration reached my brain. I hated myself for not having known, for being insensitive, impervious. I had seen him only twice when he was last home on leave, for his wife had completely monopolized him, and had taken him away to Cornwall, where he was greatly bored. I sympathized with her, but I was terribly sorry for Alan. And that was his last leave—in rooms on the Cornish coast, during a rainy month, with a woman for whom he felt pity but not one atom of love, who irritated him, and to whom he had nothing to say.

At least she never experienced the thing she most dreaded. She kept him, outwardly, to the end. Richard received a letter from her in answer to his letter of condolence, in which she said:

"Our last weeks together were perfect. He spent almost his whole leave with me in Cornwall, and it was the happiest time of our lives."

She knew—she must have known—how untrue this was, but she was able to keep her pride and her sense of possession intact.

I wondered if there would ever be an end to sadness, to losses. But in some ways I was much happier. I made friends at the hospital. The matron was made of flesh and blood instead of ice and iron, and the sisters and other helpers were agreeable and easy to get on with. I grew very fond of a lovely girl of twenty-one named Theo Brotherton, who had made her debut in the season that was closed by the war. She arrived each day in her own car, and was clearly a child of fortune. Her parents had a large house in town and two country places, and the contrast between her life and mine amused us both. She thought mine must be a thrilling existence. How lovely to live alone in rooms and be entirely independent! How marvellous to be able to write for papers and magazines! How lucky to have seen so much of the world! How exciting to be working on a novel! What was it about?

She was impulsive, demonstrative, eager to be loved. She longed to marry, and could hardly wait for the time to come—but at the moment she was in love with any and every well-built male in uniform. She had a vivid colour that came and went, and dark, ardent, liquid eyes. She was very tall and full of youthful grace, and at times gambolled and played like a charming puppy. She almost entirely conquered my reticence, and made me tell her as much as I would of my affairs and told me rather more than she should, I thought, of her own. I had never met anyone who so longed to give herself, who was so ardent and so confiding. Brains she had not; but I think brains would have spoilt her. I began to realize how much I had missed the society of my own

151

sex. She had an elder sister named Alix, who was nursing at a base hospital in France, and when she came home on leave I met her, and liked her at once.

Alix was deeply interested in spiritualism, and was in constant communication, she said, with a man who had been killed, and whom she had loved. She had done automatic writing ever since her childhood, and wrote things that astonished everybody about matters of which she could have had no previous knowledge. Many a time I have seen all expression leave her face, seen her hand and arm grow rigid, her fingers, holding the pencil, look like the cramped fingers of a paralytic, while she covered sheets of paper with all kinds of strange scribblings. One day she wrote what was clearly a message for me and signed it "Alan," in writing that was very like his. I had told Theo a little about Alan and now wished I had not, for it made me suspicious. The message, however, was remarkable, and concerned something of which neither she nor Alix had any knowledge at all. It read:

"Tell Marna the Wind from the South blew a day too late."

The books I had sent him—*South Wind* was one of them—arrived the day after he was killed, and in view of this fact the message was startling and highly circumstantial. After that Alix and I had many talks on the subject, and she influenced me considerably. I began to think there was more in spiritualism than I had thought.

She was a handsome, sombre girl of my own age, and experienced from time to time moments of extreme exaltation and clairvoyance. She was as indifferent to men—as men—as Theo was ardent and curious, and told me that her feelings for the man who was killed had been on a plane "higher" than the ordinary plane, and that she had been in love only with his mind and spirit. I think she believed this, but I have never been sure how far Alix—who was the soul of honesty—was yet capable of deceiving herself.

The two sisters interested me greatly, and my life began to change from the time I first knew them. I grew fond, too, of their cheerful, placid mother, and their gloomy, delicate, kindly father, Sir Quentin Brotherton, a banker and an amateur astronomer. I met their friends, wore Alix's dresses when my own were insufficient—as they usually were—and began to lose my diffidence. They were optimistic, courageous people for the most part, without imagination— Sir Quentin had it, and along certain lines, Alix, but Lady Brotherton and most of her friends were, I used to think, like agreeable and well-bred peasants, without imagination and without nerves. Their thoughts never went beyond the here and now, their

153

talk was unstimulating, soothing and conventional. During air raids—I experienced many at their house, as they lived near me, and I used to fly there for companionship the instant the warnings sounded— their calm self-control amazed me.

"Oh, that's miles away," they would say, after a dull explosion that made me shudder.

"Yes," I would answer, "I know, but it's some· where. It isn't my body that's been blown to bits, but it's *some* body." And I would picture blood-stained walls and pavements, and flying limbs, and feel sick.

"There are millions of houses in London; why should they hit this one?"

"It isn't that, it isn't that. . . ."

And when the "All Clear" signals sounded again I thought of the ambulances rushing through the dark to this or that ruined street, and the groans and cries—no, there was nothing of the Spartan in me, nothing. Violence is and always will be anathema to me.

When America came into the war I was an object of great interest at the hospital. What would and could America do? What would the allies in America allow her to do? Could the troops ever get across the Atlantic, which was swarming with submarines? What did I think of President Wilson? Was it true that he was pro-German? I assured them

that nothing could possibly exceed my own ignorance
of all these things, and that to have spent an obscure youth in America did not enable me to speak
with authority on such high matters.

I spent my holidays in the summer of 1917 at the
Brothertons' country house in the Lake District, near
Grasmere, and away from the crowds, the raids, the
talk, the constant and ever-present signs of war, it
seemed like heaven. There I found grass and cool
water, wild-flowers, lovely hills and heather—the first
heather I had ever seen—peaty streams, lonely up-
lands, quiet sheep, all the things I loved and had
lost for so long. And there, staying in the house,
I first met Roland. I will call him only that, instead of giving him a fictitious surname, and were
I to invent one it would not suit him.

He had lately been invalided home from Mesopotamia, and was at the War Office, his health impaired
by fever and a bullet wound in the lungs. He was
spending a fortnight's holiday at the Brothertons' and
it seemed as much like paradise to him as it did to
me. I thought him a possible suitor of Alix's at
first—Theo was too young—but he was a suitor of
neither. He was really Sir Quentin's friend, and
admired Theo far more than her elder sister, whose
mysticism and psychic faculties repelled him. He
disliked her "superiority" to ordinary sexual rela-
tionships, and her constant talk of "mind" and

"spirit," and argued with her a good deal. He was sometimes a little brutal, I thought, but she did not mind. She was always ready to splinter her cold, pure lances against the great Rock of Gibraltar of sex, which, in some obscure way, she felt was inimical to her. She was incapable of understanding it, and so hated it.

Her best friends, with one great exception, were always women, and toward them she was sympathetic and affectionate. She adored Theo, her amorous sister, but was a little disgusted at times by that young woman's very frank and natural proclivities. Between them I thought a good deal more about sex than I ever had before. I had always taken it for granted—or ever since its secrets were first revealed to me, at fifteen, by a painstaking governess—(my mother declined to undertake this task)—but I now saw it as a Problem. And I knew that for me, as for Theo, though perhaps not in the same way, it was the breath of life. Without men, without men's company, talk, admiration, love, I was starved. I loved their voices, their presence, their way of doing things, of thinking. I, too, longed to marry, but it seemed I had only to become fond of a man in order to lose him, by death or in some less violent way. Only Richard remained, and my friendship for him would have satisfied even Alix. I could have married several of the officers at the hospital. When they were away from its restrictions they came and looked me up and asked me out to dinner and the theatre, and made war-time proposals of marriage; desperate, foolish, impulsive. They wanted something, someone to cling to, to pass their names on to, to come back to; they wanted the violence of marriage, of possession, to counteract as long as it might the violence of war, eternal and never-ending war. They wanted to crowd as much as they could of action, of love, of finality, into what remained to them of life. These were natural things, understandable things, but their love was not sufficiently personal to me. It was too much the product of the time and circumstances, and, much as I pitied them, I knew they would go from me to someone else very soon, and that I need not and must not involve myself. There had been a Canadian, sentimental and pathetic, an officer in the Ghurkas, a flying man who had crashed after bringing down his tenth enemy 'plane, a very young sapper; they came and went, a procession of infinite pathos— men whom war, the great cruel forger, had tried to turn into machines, and whose humanity so piteously rebelled, so ached for expression.

Roland was different. He had come out of the war like a swimmer out of the sea, tired, but unchanged. What he had thought and felt before the war he thought and felt now. He had gone through it gravely and unhurriedly, clutching at nothing. If he were killed he would be killed exactly as he was. He had already lived a good deal. His tempo in the war was the same as his tempo in peace. War was an unfortunate happening, and one lost one's best friends, good fellows such as one would never meet again. He had no animosities and hated propaganda, but supposed it was necessary for the transforming of an exceedingly peaceful nation into a warlike one. He was not brilliant, he did not fascinate me, I never lost my head about him, but he was suddenly an important factor in my life. I was thirty. It was time for me to think seriously about marriage. The war could not go on for ever. I was tired to death of feeling myself at the mercy of circumstances.

He was very little interested in my writing and somewhat dampened my own enthusiasm for it. He read the manuscript of my unfinished novel and was not impressed. He said he thought my talents might be for journalism or perhaps for painting—he had seen none of my work and knew nothing about art— but he did not think they were for fiction. As no one else had seen the manuscript except Richard— who liked everything I wrote—I was impressed and somewhat chagrined by what he said.

He began to make love to me very directly and unsubtly before we had been there a week. In those surroundings and in the mood I was in I was ready to listen to him. Once again I felt the old triumph, the old thrill, the old fascinated curiosity as to how he would affect me, how I affected him. We used to climb the round green hills, and sit in the heather, and day after day we grew to know and like each other better. He was substantial, safe, less reliable, mentally, than Alan—or I thought less of his mentality—but more dependable as an individual, and far, far more conventional. He had the simple Englishman's ideas about women. There were good women who put chastity above everything else, and unfortunate women (he would not call them bad) who did not. And yet he liked women to be womanly, to have strong emotions, to love whole-heartedly, but only within the bonds of matrimony. In a changing, blood-drenched world he seemed to me as firm as a rock in a quicksand. His faults became virtues. I wrote to Richard:

"I think he is going to want to marry me—I perceive all the symptoms—and I think I may want to marry him. I'm sick of episodes, Richard, of things that change. I'm sick of myself. I want a home— I've never had one. Roland isn't at all well off, but after the poverty I've had I'm not afraid of that kind. I want, in the most weak and feminine way, to be looked after and protected. I think he's the sort of man you'd like. I think you'd call him 'sound.' I refuse to believe that it will make any change in our friendship. I owe everything to you;

159

I even owe my being here to you, but oh, how I want a life of my own, a home of my own! Tell me you'll be glad—or at least reconciled—if I marry. Tell me you won't mind too much."

Roland seemed to me so clearly my "fate" that I made little effort to escape him. The time, the place, the man—it was natural and inevitable that I should succumb. He was a tall man, well—perhaps too solidly—built, with regular and unremarkable features, dark hair growing thin, blue eyes that had an expression at once candid and simple, and a small, military moustache. Theo called him "England, Home and Duty," and it was very apt. He had none of Alan's rebellious fire, none of Richard's fine taste, nor his rich and cultivated mind. He was ready and anxious to "settle down," and in those catastrophic days the expression was not distasteful to me. I thought of a house with a garden, of a library, of possible children, of peace (if the war should ever end) and calm security. I thought of the devotion of a good and admirable man, whom I would make as happy as I could. In fact, I thought at that time as conventionally as he did, more conventionally than I have ever thought, before or since, and for this the war was responsible.

The day before he was to return to London it rained all day. In the afternoon Lady Brotherton was lying down in her room and Theo and Sir Quentin had motored in to Windermere. Alix had returned, two days before, to her base hospital in France. Roland and I were writing letters in the sitting-room in a somewhat oppressive silence. I was very conscious of him, and conscious of his feelings toward me. My back was turned to him, but I was fully aware of his every movement. To sit in the same quiet room with a man who is in love but has not yet declared his love is like waiting for a storm to break on a hot and sultry day. One longs for it and dreads it. I had thought about him for a week, constantly, and was as nervous as a cat. What would I say—do—when the time came? One half of my mind said, "This is the man," the other half said, "Not yet, not yet." To that half I replied, "But if not now, when? I'm thirty, thirty, thirty, you fool! Incredible as it may seem, I was born in 1887. If not now, when? And whom?"

I sat writing to my mother, and in the middle of my letter he crossed the room to me, and I felt his hands press my shoulders, and his lips the back of my neck. I sprang up, and saw that he was pale and much moved.

"I couldn't help it—I couldn't sit in the same room with you any longer, and not—I'm so in love with you—Marna—you're going to marry me. You know it. You're going to marry me."

He took me in his arms and kissed me violently,

161

and repeated, over and over again, that I was going to marry him. He asked me no questions, but took complete command of the situation. He said I loved him, and I believed I did. I finally admitted that I did, and a weight seemed to drop from my shoulders.

"You're mine and I'm yours," he said between his kisses. "I knew it a week ago. You're mine and I'm yours. We'll tell the others to-night. I want to tell everybody. I love and adore you, and you love me. We belong to each other."

He was powerful, convincing, dominating. I assented to everything. I was happy to be loved again. Yes, I loved him. Yes, I would marry him. Yes, we would tell the others that evening. Yes, my mother would be delighted. Physically he was attractive to me, and I responded. It was good to be in his arms, to feel myself held by a muscular, powerful and determined man, good to have arrived at a goal, to feel I should not be alone any more. Here was the end of doubts, fears, loneliness, the end of drifting. I now had a place in life, like other people. I was marrying an old friend of the Brothertons. They would approve and be glad. I felt safe and happy, and my emotions were deeply stirred. We could hardly tear ourselves from each other's arms at the sound of Lady Brotherton's descending footsteps.

They did approve, and Theo was ecstatic.

"It's almost as good as getting married myself. How lovely that it happened here, and through us! Oh, Marna, how I envy you! Oh, do get married soon, soon!"

But when I lay in bed and tried to sleep, the wild animal that was my love of independence, stirred a little, and was restless.

Roland wrote to his father, who lived in Florence from motives of economy, and then forwarded me his delighted reply. The very word "marriage" seemed to give people pleasure, it seemed. Why? There were plenty of unhappy ones about. I began to feel a little disgusted with the facile emotions the prospect of my own marriage aroused, with the sentimental utterances, with the view, which most people seemed to hold, that one had only to marry to be radiantly, exquisitely happy. I needed opposition— and I got it, from Richard.

His letter came as I was about to return to London, to begin work again.

"Marna, what are you doing? Who is this man? His name means nothing whatever to me. You aren't in love with him. I don't believe it. Eighteen months ago you were in love with Morisan. I feel certain you are making a mistake. I must see you, and meet him. I am terribly distressed and grieved. I cannot allow you to act so precipitately. If it is poverty that is driving you into this marriage, I will give you half my fortune. When are you coming back? Please go no further until I have seen you. I ask this, as your best friend. I insist on it. All my love. Richard."

He would come to it gradually—he must. He would feel differently when he had met Roland. But I promised that I would at least not allow myself to be officially engaged, or announce my engagement (it was Roland who wished this to be done) until I had seen him again. The two men were already antagonistic. I had only to mention Richard to see a look of disquiet on Roland's face; I had only to mention Roland to make Richard depressed and unhappy.

"Why do you want to marry now? The whole country may be starving in a few weeks if the submarines continue to sink food ships at the rate they are doing. Why don't you at least wait till the war is over? Are you so madly in love that you must rush into it headlong? I don't believe it. You're tired of living alone, and in those rooms. We'll make some other arrangement. You know I've wanted to for a long time. You and your mother must take a flat together. That will be my affair. Will you do this? Why not, why not?"

I told him I was thirty, and it was time I married. Also that he had done more than enough for me.

164

"Thirty? What of that? Thirty is nothing. I'm fifty. Oh, Marna, don't do it, don't do it!"

At last I was able to bring them together. We dined, the three of us, at Richard's invitation. I was nervous and watchful. From the moment the men met and shook hands I felt they were opposed to one another. Roland felt for Richard something of the distrust the soldier, the man of action, often feels for the diplomat, while Richard hardly smiled, or if he did, smiled only at me. Nevertheless he spared no effort to make the dinner a success. He soon discovered that Roland cared little for such things as silver, tapestries, primitives; that he did not read poetry and knew almost nothing of music; so he talked chiefly about politics and war. He was not displeased, I felt, at the thought that I must surely realize what a Philistine I was thinking of marrying, and this put me on the defensive at once.

Even about games—and both were cricket enthusiasts—they found little on which to agree. I could feel that they drew further and further apart as dinner went on. Roland disliked a certain Cabinet Minister and disapproved of his schemes. Richard with punctilious accuracy proved to him that he was insufficiently and wrongly informed. Roland spoke well of a certain general. Richard pointed out a serious failing. I soon saw that the battle was lost as far as I was concerned, and the thought distressed

165

me, for under other circumstances I believed they would have liked each other. Richard would have said that Roland was a good fellow and a good soldier; Roland would have said that Richard was the type of man to whom England owed much of her greatness.

I had the next afternoon free and, on hearing so, Richard said he was coming to see me at four o'clock. Immediately Roland reminded me that I had promised to go with him to meet an aunt of his, but that of course I must do as I pleased. Nothing definite had been arranged, and I knew this, so I said I would go with him the week after, and that, as I was dining with him that evening, I would see Richard in the afternoon.

"Well?" I asked, as he was driving me home.

"Well," he answered, "I know what you want to know. Oh, I know he's been a good friend to you, but he seems to think he owns you. I'm afraid he and I will never see eye to eye. He's in love with you, of course. The whole position is very difficult, and I think you'd better try to end it, as kindly as you can."

"That," I said, "I will never do."

He did not argue with me any further then. We were too newly engaged for him to wish to talk to me when he could kiss me, and we drove the rest of the way in each other's arms.

166

Sixteen to Forty

Richard and I had tea in my sitting-room the next afternoon, then walked in Regent's Park.

"My dear, if he cared for the things you care for, it would be different. Will he encourage you to paint, to write? You know he won't. He cares nothing for those things. I think he is a brave fellow, and I have no doubt he is a good soldier, but he is not for you."

"I'll paint whenever I get the chance," I told him, "and as for writing, I'll have to write. I'll have to make some money. So there's that incentive. Richard, he'll try to make me happy, he really cares very much for me, he's a lovable man, and a dependable man. I know I'm not making a mistake."

"I know you are," he said, quietly. "I see his good qualities, but I think I should call him—" he hesitated. "No, I must not overstate what I feel. I will say this. I would have chosen someone for you with finer perceptions, someone more intellectual, more—I dislike the word, but I use it in its best sense —more cultured."

"But, Richard, darling, you've never chosen anyone for me, and it's extremely unlikely that you ever would. Tell me honestly, do you know a man, have you ever known a man, whom you should like me to marry?"

He pondered this, and finally admitted with perfect honesty, "No." Then, with an odd little smile that was both humorous and wistful, he said, "I would like you to have married me."

"But that's out of the question, you dear. Richard, really, I think it's better for me to marry. I do. You know what I'm like. You know that I'm emotional, passionate, full of feeling. I'm starved. I must love someone. If I don't marry soon I'll go off the rails as they call it. I can't go on living like this indefinitely."

Again he was silent, and for some time. Arm in arm we walked slowly under the trees. At last he said, "I suppose you must marry, then. But I wish it were someone else. I should be less unhappy, I think, if it were someone else."

"There is no one else," I said, "and there never will be, now. If I wait for the perfect thing, I'll wait for ever."

He looked at me with tragic eyes.

"If only it might have been you and I, my dear. If only it might!"

I made no answer, and he expected none. He said presently,

"If it must be, it must. I have made my protest. I don't like it. I don't think it will make you happy, though perhaps you will get something else out of it —experience—knowledge. But there it is. You have made up your mind. I will protest no more."

"Will it make any difference," I asked, "between

you and me? That is the only thing I dread. Will you feel differently towards me? I couldn't bear that. It will make no difference to me, I promise you. I swear it."

He said finally and after consideration that he thought it would make no difference, that he would try not to let it. I shall never forget that afternoon in Regent's Park. He was wearing a shabby old blue suit, glossy here and there from age and brushing, and in his button-hole shone a resplendent flower. His too sensitive face looked tired and drawn, his eyes haggard from overwork. He always reminded me a little of the White Knight in *Alice in Wonderland,* his face had that same pathetic gentleness. He had the heart of a child, and the mind and brain of a statesman. I loved him, and how differently from the way I loved anyone else! I had told him so again and again, but I think women are capable of more kinds of love than men are, and I do not think he understood how I could love him and at the same time love someone else, though it was clear and simple enough to me.

He took me home at half-past six, and I dressed to go out with Roland.

I tried to persuade Roland that evening that it was better not to marry till the end of the war was at least in sight, and in the autumn of 1917 no man could say when that time might be, but he saw no reason for waiting. We decided, then, on a day in November, and I saw my engagement announced in the *Times* with something of a shock, though I expected it. It seemed to me absurd to announce an engagement in time of war, but Roland had been through nearly three years of war and I had not, and if he wished it, I saw no reason to oppose it.

My mother was delighted. She had no doubt at all that I was doing the right thing, and the thought of a son-in-law who was a soldier, an Englishman, and a D.S.O., enchanted her, and made her feel that everything had happened for the best. She was to live with us half the year and to spend the other half in whatever way she chose. I began to look at unfurnished flats, and when I considered the long leases—eight years, ten years, fifteen years, my heart sometimes sank. I was very fond of Roland, if I did not love him wildly; physically he was, as I have said, attractive to me, and it was the fact that he was much less attractive to me mentally that made me wonder and doubt a little. But I assured myself that once I was married, once the thing was done, I should feel differently.

In October Richard fell ill and was obliged to take a holiday. Bolsover House, since 1916, had been a convalescent home for wounded soldiers, so he had to go elsewhere. My approaching marriage filled him with dread, and he implored me to let

him see as much of me as possible before the time
came. When the doctor ordered him away he refused to leave London unless my mother and I went
with him, and begged us to let him take us to an
inn in Dorset, kept by two old servants of the family.
I told Roland that I thought we should go, and I
was astonished at the storm it aroused.

He knew that Richard and I had things in common
that he and I had not, and resented it. He was
bitterly jealous, and in his jealousy he was un-
generous.

He was sorry Richard had been ill, but he would
soon be all right, and there was no need for me to
worry. Why should he not go alone? Frankly, he
said, he did not understand what Richard's position
in my life was going to be.

"I hope he will continue to be my best friend."

"I should have thought I was that."

I told him again—I had told him often before—
how much I owed to Richard, and begged him to be
reasonable.

"It's not very much for him to ask. I can get
leave from the hospital. It will make Richard very
happy, and my mother hasn't been away from Putney
for two years—besides, I want to do it."

He said there were a hundred things in connection
with our wedding that we had not discussed yet.

"Can't we discuss them now?" I asked.

"They'll come up later on."

"My dear, a simple little wedding like ours doesn't require much preparation. We've decided on a service flat for the present, so there's nothing to buy, and everything else is settled. And we'll only be away for ten days or so."

He hated the idea, and could not reconcile himself to it.

"I know he's done his best to persuade you not to marry me. I know he'd prevent it if he could. I don't like the idea of your having for an intimate friend a man who dislikes me. I don't see why I should sacrifice myself to him. If he liked me, it might be different."

I made up my mind that I would not give in. I did not want to be dominated in this way. I had a mind of my own, reasoning powers of my own, and I wished to be allowed to use them. Also it was the first request Richard had ever made me.

I told Roland to think it over and try to see my side of it, and to ring me up in the morning. He counselled me to do likewise, but in the morning our minds were unchanged.

"I'm going, Roland. I've told Richard I would. If I didn't go I'd have to say why, and I don't want to do that."

"Well, under the circumstances I think it would be

best to postpone the wedding indefinitely," he replied.

The next day we went to Dorset, and he did not
come to see us off. I knew how unhappy he was
making himself, and I was sorry. I wrote him a
long letter and tried to reassure him, and said that
he would hear from me every day. In reply I received an injured letter from him.

"I have no influence over you, evidently. Only
Richard has that. You ought to be marrying him
instead of me. You are like Alix. The word 'friendship' seems to have some value for you that love
has not. Frankly I don't understand a friendship of
that sort between a man and a woman, and I don't
believe in it. Richard is in love with you and knows
it very well. You are in love with him and don't
know it. It's a poor prospect for me."

I could not believe he was serious, and wrote him
an answer immediately. Three of the ten days were
already gone. I should be back in a week. Meanwhile Richard improved daily. We took walks along
the delightful lanes, drove, sometimes, in a dog-cart
that belonged to the inn—motoring for pleasure in
those days being denied to us—read, talked and slept
deeply and peacefully. My mother was as delighted
as a school-girl at being there with Richard, and I
was much struck by her youthful spirits, her elasticity, and her capacity for enjoying to the full such

fortunate moments as came her way. It saddened me to think how few there were, and how little I had been able to do for her. The Lawtons had done everything, I almost nothing. (Much as I appreciated their lovable, excellent qualities, their goodness and generosity, I was no more drawn to them than I was at first, nor could I, however hard I tried, make myself fonder of them.) My mother had kept her youthful figure, and although her face was more lined and her hair greyer, she was still a pretty woman. There was something naturally and unaffectedly good and simple about her. In some ways she had never grown up, and I felt much the older of the two. She missed my father very much, but I think she was happier, living placidly and quietly with the Lawtons, than she had been with him. She had been so often frightened and distressed that I think their happier, earlier days together were somewhat obscured by the anxieties that came later.

When I got back to London Roland met me with a sort of ultimatum. He looked upon Richard as an enemy, and was convinced that Richard looked upon him as such. Under the circumstances he could not and would not agree to my seeing him. He was willing to give up anything or anyone for me. If I were unwilling to do as much for him it showed him exactly where he stood, and he thought we had better end it.

I implored and argued. I tried to kiss him into common sense, but he was immovable. If I were not in love with Richard, what he asked was not too much. If I were—

In love! Was one either wholly indifferent to a man or in love with him? Was affection, gratitude, to count for nothing? I told him plainly enough that I was not in love with Richard, but that I loved him dearly and would not dream of giving him up, or promising not to see him.

"Then it's all over," he said. "If you decide differently, let me know. I'll wait."

"You'll wait a good while, my dear, if you wait for that."

"Very well, I'll wait."

"Oh," I cried, "why are you so afraid? Why don't you make me love you better than anyone else in the world? That's your job. And you could do it."

"The dice are loaded against me from the start. Richard is first with you now. I want to start fair."

I was as immovable as he, and he went away. In a day or two he wrote me a formal letter, releasing me from my engagement.

This childish behaviour enraged me, but I could do nothing more. And yet, in spite of my anger, my affection for him seemed to grow. I wrote to say that our engagement could hang fire for the moment, and the wedding could be postponed, but received no reply. I knew how he was suffering, but short of a complete surrender there seemed no help for it. His love I did not doubt for an instant. He was a conventional man, feared a rival, and dreaded Richard's influence over me. He would rather suffer than give way.

I believed, however, that he would come round, but weeks went by and he gave no sign. The Brothertons no longer saw him, and I completely lost touch with him. I often walked through St. James's Park and along Whitehall in the hope of seeing his tall, soldierly, uniformed figure coming out of or going into the War Office, but I never did. My feelings about him were unchanged, and I was very unhappy, but work kept me from brooding over it. Richard, of course, said I was well out of it, but he was tactful on the whole, and grieved that he had been the cause of our disagreement.

As the winter passed I thought of him constantly, and knew that he thought of me. In February I finished my novel and sent it to Mr. Lenyard, who told me he felt sure he could place it, if not at once, the moment the war was over.

But the war did not look in the least like being over. In January there had been a terrible air raid, two hundred and thirty-three people being killed and injured. Merchant ships were still being sunk, and a hospital ship was torpedoed in the Channel. There was deadlock along the Western Front—though there was activity enough in other theatres of war—and still that awful outpouring of blood went on. Then, suddenly, the Great German Offensive was begun, filling the most optimistic with dread, and on March 21st there opened the Second Battle of the Somme.

Then the wounded were sent back to receive fresh wounds, those whose lives had been miraculously preserved for three terrible years were now to lose them, the awful, final effort was required of everyone, either of sacrifice or endurance, and Roland was ordered to France at little more than forty-eight hours' notice.

He wrote me a letter of good-bye, and for me it was pure agony. I got it on Tuesday; on Wednesday he was to go. He said nothing in it about seeing me, but I read his awful longing between the lines. I tried to ring him up at the War Office, but it was hopeless. He was not at his small flat in Duke Street, for I tried repeatedly to telephone, and got no reply. I could not work, I hardly knew what I was doing, so I told the matron what ailed me, and she let me off for the day. I got out of my uniform and into street clothes in ten minutes, and took a taxi to Duke Street, meaning to wait on the steps if necessary. But as I got out of my cab he drove up in another surrounded by kit-bags and haversacks, things that had been stored away since his return.

"Mama!" He stared at me with hungry, searching eyes.

"Oh, my dear, I've been trying to ring you up all day. You must have known I'd want to see you—have to see you—Oh, you idiot!—you idiot!"

I was crying. He had never seen me cry before, and the sight seemed to give him comfort and hope.

"Come upstairs. I've got to get ready. You can help me. Where's that porter?"

An old man came up from the basement and helped him to carry his things up the stairs.

"Off again, sir? I thought they'd done with you. My son went back this morning, with his head hardly healed up from the last time. Why don't them as makes the war go to the war?"

The door of the flat closed and we were alone. I was as hungry for his kisses as he was for mine, and the thought of the next day made our reunion more moving and poignant, and greatly intensified our emotions. For me, that day and the fourth of August were the most terrible of the whole war. That Roland, with his injured lung and his recurrent fevers, should once more be hurled into the furnace seemed to me ghastly beyond words.

He broke down and cried that he had been wrong, and a fool. All this time we might have been married, living together—oh, God! What a fool he

178

had been! And now it was too late, we had had nothing but misery and emptiness—it was all his fault——

"Oh, Roland, no, I was to blame, too. I should have given in. I should have compromised in some way. It's *you* who have suffered and fought and risked your life for months on end, and been through hell. I should have thought of this. I should have foreseen it."

"Never mind—never mind—it's too late now. We were both wrong—but you're here now. How long can you stay with me?"

"As long as you like. I'm not going back to the hospital till to-morrow morning."

"Shall we dine here, or go out? We can have a little dinner here, but it won't be good."

"No, let's dine here. I want to be able to cry if I feel like it. I don't care what we have to eat, or if we don't have anything."

He said he would order a little dinner for eight o'clock, and get his packing done first. Then we could talk. He had let his soldier servant go to Kent to say good-bye to his family there, and he was not returning till the early morning, so we were quite alone in the flat. Nothing had any importance for me that evening, nothing but Roland's going, and Roland. Man, the Victim, seemed epitomized in the person of Roland, who was to offer his body once again to stop a break in a wall. The fury of the

179

German push was frightful, the loss of life appalling, everything that had been gained seemed about to be lost, and people talked of the Germans getting to Calais. I reproached myself bitterly for having sacrificed him to Richard, foolish and unnecessary as the quarrel had been. It was the politicians, after all, who could have stopped the war and did not, who talked of giving Germany a thorough beating, talked of victory and glory, and shut their eyes to the slaughter. And I—I who stayed safely at home, what had I done but add to a burden that was already too heavy, to a debt that I was already incapable of repaying?

That was my mood that evening.

It was a sad little meal, and I could not eat. We talked, with forced, false cheerfulness, of marrying as soon as he came back. Roland was calm, sane, sparing of embraces, as though he feared to put too great a strain upon his endurance. I had never liked him better. All the things I admired most in him were uppermost that night, the things he lacked were of no importance. If there were limits to his flexibility, to his mental powers, there were no limits to his splendid courage.

He looked at his watch at last.

"It's eleven o'clock, my dearest, I must take you home."

"Why? Why should I go home at eleven to-night,

or even twelve, as though it were any other night?"

"You can stay till twelve, then."

"Why do you want to end it? Is it because you want to sleep?"

"Good God, no! How can I sleep?"

"Then let me stay as long as I please, and don't talk about time. I like your conventionality and propriety, Roland, except at times like this, and then I hate it. It's no one's business but mine and yours if I choose to stay all night."

"Marna, don't talk nonsense."

"I mean it. What does it matter? Is it Mrs. Grundy or God you're afraid of? Surely she's in bed and asleep, and he's too busy listening to President Wilson and the Kaiser and Mr. Lloyd George, who are all invoking him and claiming his attention, to bother about little pawns like us."

"Leave God out of it. You are precisely the same kind of woman to me whether there's a war on or not, and you're the kind of woman a man takes care of. I'll take care of you to-night as I would any other night."

"And I'll take care of you to-night, my dearest, but in a much kinder way. Close your eyes and put your head here, and I'll whisper something to you. I'm not going home. I'm going to stay here with you."

It was not I who conquered him in the end, but himself who conquered him—the self he suppressed with such an iron hand broke loose, and I rejoiced that it did. As for me, I had made up my mind that I would send him away happy and certain of me, that I would make up to him as far as I was able for what he had been—through his own stubbornness —deprived of, and that I must not let this end as other things had ended, in nothingness. I had had enough and more than enough of episodes, of experiences that left me as they found me, with only an added memory, and when I knew, definitely and finally, that I must let nothing stand in the way of complete surrender, the sense of release, mental and physical, was overwhelming.

That night I persuaded myself and him that I utterly loved him, that I loved him in all the ways that it was possible for a woman to love a man, and that I was his entirely and irrevocably, and without a single regret.

CHAPTER VIII

I N 1922 Alix Brotherton had been married for a year and a half to a French scientist named Pierre Morin, who was an important member of the French Society of Psychical Research. She had first met him at her Base Hospital in France during the war, and had deeply impressed him by her psychic gifts. Regarding her first as an interesting subject, he presently fell in love with her, or, at any rate, made up his mind to marry her, and after repeatedly refusing him, she eventually, to the surprise of her family and friends, accepted him, and they were married in Paris. He was a widower of nearly sixty, of brilliant mental powers, but in appearance highly unattractive. He was short, stout, bearded, hirsute, gross. I was ready to believe then that she really cared nothing for the physical relationship, and that she had entered into some sort of pact with him, of which she never spoke. At any rate, she kept her virginal outlook on life and her sombre reticence intact, and was as unmatronly as a married woman could well be. She worked side by side with her husband and seemed as interested in psychic research as he was himself. She submitted, in the company of some of his friends, to tests of her own powers, which now included mediumship of a high order.

They lived in a small house near the Parc Monceau, and there, eighteen months after Roland's death, I went to visit them. I had been to Paris only once since my art school days, and that was when I went there with Roland in 1920. We had planned a trip to the Pyrenees, but he suffered so from the effects of the first part of the journey that we gave up all idea of continuing it, and returned to London and to his doctor there. After that we never left England, and in April, 1921, he died.

Theo married Cyril Greswall, the son of a well-known politician. He was the same age as Theo and had served in the Navy, though he did not remain in it after the war was over. Instead he married Theo and went into politics. He was a good-looking and very likeable young man, but his only qualifications for a political career were leisure, a certain amount of money, and a good character. They were a delightful, happy-go-lucky pair, and wildly in love. Theo bore him girl twins in the first year of their marriage, and her ardour turned, as it so often does, to mother-love; her one idea seemed to be to bear children as often as possible and be with them as much as possible. When she was not occupied in this way she gave Cyril considerable help in his constituency by appearing in the doorways of the poor with a smiling child in each hand and, by her simple and disarming loveliness, winning a surprising number of voters to the Liberal Cause. She remained my admiring and devoted friend, and I was very fond of them all, and was godmother to one of the twins. Alix and her curious marriage interested me more, however, and I was glad of an opportunity of visiting them.

At first the meetings of the Society fascinated me, and I took a keen interest in the reports of the phenomena investigated, and in the tests and experiments. I was glad to know what was going on in that secluded and significant circle, but after two weeks of it I found it began to pall. I came to the conclusion that the human mind possesses powers of which we know extremely little, and to which we have not yet the key, and I felt it was highly improbable that we should know more in my lifetime. I entirely approved of the investigations and of the classifying and cataloguing of facts, but I decided that if what I saw and heard was true—and it undoubtedly was— we were a very long way indeed from the explanation, and where almost anything seemed possible, surprise and wonder became incongruous and stupid. And as soon as I could no longer be legitimately surprised, I began to be bored. Alix and Pierre Morin themselves interested me far more than the phe-

185

nomena they investigated. It was a curious marriage. I never saw a caress pass between them. They lived in separate rooms. Alix was more like his secretary than his wife. I wondered if he had a mistress and Alix knew of it, and if it were all part of the arrangement. Anything seemed probable but that he could have lived like a monk under the same roof with a handsome and desirable woman, who was his wife and yet not his wife.

In this unusual menage I met Chester Dellamere, an American writer. He had come to Paris to meet Pierre Morin, and find out from him, if he could, what was the evidence for a future life, for he hated the thought of death, of extinction, and feared it.

I liked him, and he brought back to my mind all the happy things that had been part of my childhood and early youth in America, and made the sad, unhappy things recede. He knew the North West, he knew California, he knew New York, and we found much to talk about. I no longer allowed myself to be taken to lectures and "sittings," and as he wished only to discuss the subject with Pierre Morin and not to investigate on his own account, we were left much together, for he was staying at a hotel near by, and knew no one else in Paris.

He was a thin, bony, sallow man, with a clean-shaven face, unremarkable features and a brilliant smile. He had read my books, and I had read his essays and one of his biographies. He thought I could do much better work than I had done so far, and asked why I had written, as my first novel, one that had such an obviously popular appeal.

"To make money, of course," I answered. If he could have seen that hideous bedroom at Mrs. Smythson's, if he could have glanced back over all the years of poverty that had nearly stifled me!

"Well, it wasn't a bad book at that," he said. "The girl was real. The life here in Paris at the art school was real. I enjoyed it, but——"

"It made hundreds of pounds for me, and helped me to take care of a mother and an invalid husband. So did the second book, which I wrote after I was married, and which was filmed. The third book you'll admit was better."

"It was good. I didn't know you'd been so poor. Tell me about your life."

"No. Not yet. One of these days, perhaps."

"You *must* tell me. Promise me you will."

"I will one day. I promise."

I liked his dark, keen face, his lively interest in everything, his knowledge of history, which was very considerable. At times he irritated me, but that was a little later, when he fell in love. Before that I altogether liked him.

Together we went to the Louvre—memories of Ella Steevens, now living in the North of England with her sister!—to the Cluny—memories of Edouard, now comfortably married, and a father, and fatter than ever!—to the Gustave Moreau Museum, to the Luxembourg, where I delighted in Monet, Manet, Degas, Pisarro—memories of Frank Bellamy, who had first spoken their names to me—Van Gogh, Gauguin, Faulin, Fantin-Latour. Here my hunger for brush and canvas assailed me like a gnawing disease, and I wondered why I ever did anything but paint. Bit by bit we told each other about our lives.

"How old are you?" he demanded one day, puzzled and baffled. "You seem to have lived a good deal, and yet you don't look a day over twenty-seven."

"I'm thirty-five, and don't mind owning to it."

"You can't be! Your face is as smooth as a child's, there isn't a grey hair in that charming dark head. You can't be thirty-five."

"I am. I don't know how to account for it. I suppose I was born young."

He laughed.

"I'm only thirty-seven, and I look old enough to be your father."

"You do look older than that. I'll be frank with you. I wonder why? You've had a pleasant, easy life."

"Mentally I haven't. I'm afraid of nearly everything. I'm afraid of living and I'm afraid of dying. Physical danger I don't mind particularly, if it's un-

188

avoidable. I don't think I'm a coward in that way. If I saw a child drowning I'd try to save it. I'd probably try to get people out of a burning house. What I hate is to think that death just lies there—" he pointed ahead of him—"and waits for us. That it's in front of every single one of us. What is life, anyhow, but a procession to a guillotine? The thought drives me nearly crazy sometimes. I long to escape the knife."

"Think of it as a sleep," I advised. "Think of it as night, and think how tired you'll be. They may or may not remember to call you in the morning, but I think the chances are they will."

"Do you? I wish I did. It's queer. I'm not so mad about living, but Lord! how I hate dying! I haven't got much satisfaction out of Morin. He says proof is impossible so far. Too little is known about the consciousness of the individual on this plane— in this life. Well, let's not talk about it. Why should I talk about death when I'm with you?"

"Why shouldn't you?"

"Because you're the most charming woman I ever met, and you make me think too much about living, and the benefits that might be derived from it."

"I don't mind your saying pleasant things to me if you feel you must, Chester, but I warn you, I hate mere compliments, and they spring much too easily to the lips of the American male."

189

"They only spring to my lips in your presence," he replied, "but I'll try to control them, if you say so."

We talked a good deal about Alix's marriage, and he took the same view of it that I did.

"I wonder," he mused, "if we place too much importance on the physical relationship. How important do you think it is?"

We were sitting in the Bois, on a still October day, and the brown leaves were falling all about us.

"I think it's about one-third of the whole," I said. "The mental relationship is two-thirds. But unless you have complete mental compatibility, the physical naturally assumes undue importance."

"Did you have the perfect whole?"

I had known him now for some weeks, seeing him nearly every day. We had talked frankly to each other, and I liked him sufficiently to wish him to know me, and to give him my confidence.

"No," I told him, "I did not. At the very beginning, the mental was one-third, the physical two-thirds, though possibly a good deal of that was affection. Just before the Armistice he was badly wounded for the second time, and again in the lungs, where he had been wounded before. At that time we had only been married a week. After that, his life was just one long fight with death, and we both knew it was a losing fight. He never forgave himself for having married me and exposed me to such a risk,

190

but I had every intention of marrying him, whether he came back whole or a cripple."

"If he had lived—I mean, lived as a healthy man, would it have been a happy marriage?"

"No," I confessed; "but he never knew that."

"Are you sure he didn't know it?"

"Absolutely sure."

"What made you marry him? Oh, the war, I suppose, your admiration for him, and pity. Then you had no married life at all, really?"

"Practically none."

"You'll marry again, surely," he said, looking keenly at me.

"Knowing what I know now, I won't marry any man I feel I can live without."

"What about loneliness?"

"Oh, I have my writing, and my paintings, and friends."

"Marna," he burst out, "this whole question of marriage beats me, doesn't it you? Is it a good institution, or isn't it? Is it sensible, or is it crazy? I can't make it out. If people don't care for each other, what's the good of keeping them together? If they do care for each other, they'll keep themselves together."

"It's for the children," I said. "For the family. The French know that. And it protects young people from the worst consequences of their own folly. Girls and young men would constantly be making alliances and regretting them, and there'd be no machinery for seeing that they dealt fairly with each other. In the present state of our civilization it seems to me a good thing, on the whole."

"What do you think of this so-called civilization, anyway?"

"I believe it's better than any we know of, so far."

"Then you believe in Evolution?"

"I think I do. It seems to me that everything has a tendency to right itself, to perfect itself. Like our bodies—I'm always amazed at the way they fight decay, disease, injury. They are overcome in the end, but the instinct to fight is there. Look at the way bark grows over a cut in a tree—the way our skins heal—the way we forget pain—the way strong things survive—the way beauty, perfection, attracts us—the way we instinctively seek it. The idea of Good is before our eyes all the time."

"Yes," he said, "whatever Good is."

"We seem to look forward instinctively to a Perfection we never find. Perhaps that's why we resent death—we imagine it interferes with that Discovery. And perhaps, if we only knew it, it leads to it. Even the search for food is a kind of search for Good. We never seek emptiness, illness, decay, but always their opposites. Even when we seek extinction, nothingness, it's only because it appears to us as a higher

192

Good—or a lesser Evil, which is the same thing."

"I like the word, Evolution," said Chester.

"It's the best word mankind has ever invented," I agreed. "By far the greatest word. There's a kind of deep knowledge in it, there's infinite patience in it, and a feeling about time, there's a recognition of man's smallness, and at the same time of his importance. There's hope in it, and there's a most pathetic prayer——"

But although Chester liked to start abstract discussions, he wasn't very good at going on with them, and usually changed the subject.

"Have you loved other men? You must have. Tell me. I'd like to know all about them."

"I've been fond of a good many men, but I'm afraid I've never really been in love with any. I doubt if I ever shall be now. I can't do without men, and yet I can't wholly love one. Not entirely, not without mental reservations—and that, to my mind, isn't being in love."

"You're too critical," he said.

"I can't help that. There's a moment in everyone's life, or there ought to be, when the whole organism cries out, 'Yes,' without a single dissenting voice. I'd give anything to feel that. Have you felt it?"

"Only once," he answered, "and only for six months. I married her."

"My dear Chester, why have you never told me?"

"I was ashamed to. The whole thing was so—pusillanimous—I was ashamed to confess it. But I'll tell you now. I was a poet, remember, in my early youth—or I believed I was—and when I was very young, about twenty, I went up to Vermont and stayed at a farmhouse there one summer. If you've never been to Vermont you'll have no idea how beautiful it is, but I can tell you this; it's like rural England on a big, generous, careless scale. There was a young beauty in the house—the farmer's daughter —yes, you may smile—who was built on much the same scale as Vermont. My God, she was lovely! She was luscious; a heavenly creature to look upon. She made the blood go tearing through my veins. I didn't say to myself then, as I'd say now, 'Leave her alone, you fool, she'll only bore you.' I said, 'I've got to have her.' And I did, or she me. I'm not quite sure now which is the truth of it. While I was hesitating as to how to tell her of my love, she walked into my bedroom one night in her nightdress, with a candle in her hand. Two weeks later I was married to her, though by that time I knew very well she had walked into other men's bedrooms. It didn't matter—I was out of my head—she was so marvellously lovely. She continued, however, to walk into other men's bedrooms, and at the same time she began to bore me so intolerably that I knew the time had

194

come for us to part. I don't think any man's love—
I admit it was wholly physical love—ever started at
a higher temperature and dropped to a lower one in
less time than mine did. I was disgusted with myself—not so much for my actions as for my feelings.
She spared me all difficulty by running off with a
good-looking and virile theatrical manager she met
on the train while she was travelling with me from
New York to Boston, and that ended it. I divorced
her, with the kindest feelings. She's now at Holly-
wood, I believe, playing 'dear old mother' parts in
the films. She aged very quickly. That's my shame-
ful story."

"You're very well and very luckily out of it."

He turned to me, with a look that I knew I would
soon see in his eyes, and putting a hand on my wrist,
said:

"And I've never had the least desire to try it again
till now. I don't know how much you like me, or
if your whole being will cry out 'yes,' or whether the
noes will have it, but you can be Mrs. Dellamere any
time you like. I always thought I'd marry a widow.
If you'll give me a little hope, I'll begin telling you
what I really feel about you, because so far you've
frightened it out of me."

I felt annoyed, and I think I showed it.

"Really, Chester, that's the worst approach to a
proposal of marriage that has ever come my way.

195

How disappointing of you! I like you enormously,
but I assure you I'd never dream of marrying you."

"Why not, if you like me? I'm dead serious."

"So am I."

He was chagrined.

"Did I approach the thing badly? Does it matter?
I mean it, desperately. I think you're the most wonderful woman. . . ."

He seemed to me full of unevennesses, of dis-
crepancies. He was half-cultured man-of-the-world,
and half-crude, average American male. In all matters to do with women he was wholly the latter.

"I can imagine a Yale undergraduate proposing
marriage in exactly the same way to his sister's girl
friend at a dance. 'You can be Mrs. Dellamere whenever you like.' Awful! I'm shocked. That is the
sort of thing that really does shock me. And yet, I
suppose, if I loved you, it wouldn't really matter.
Why have you no finesse in approaching a woman?
Why haven't you learnt it? It's your business to
learn it."

"I know," he admitted, "I'm no good at it. I can
dream wonderful things about a woman, but I never
say them."

"Who wants you to say them—or dream them
either? Heaven knows I'm not asking you to be sentimental. Quite the contrary. I want you to see more
clearly and sharply the person you're talking to. I'm

196

a certain sort of woman who has lived a certain sort of life, and the methods you might employ—though I hope you wouldn't—with a young girl from Tuskaloosa are not the ones you should employ with me. The trouble with you is that you can't make up your mind whether women are goddesses or rather naughty jokes, and you waver between the two points of view. You ought to have known me well enough to know that I'd be disgusted by a flippant and semihumorous proposal of marriage."

"My God! I've brought an avalanche on my head!"

"Yes, and you deserve it. You've spoilt the afternoon for me. I'm going home." I got up, and he got up, puzzled.

"Look here, are you really angry with me, or pretending?"

"A little of both," I said. We turned and walked toward the lake, a sheet of soft grey surrounded by sad browns and dull greens. "I'm really feeling cold; we sat there long enough. I'm depressed by the thought of winter. I hate winter—I hate cold. If I can afford it I'll go South after Christmas, to some quiet place along the Mediterranean where there's sun. That is, if I can bear to leave London. Where will you be? In Philadelphia?"

"I don't know. Probably. I may stay over here. Supposing I came to London, can I see something of

197

you? You evidently don't realize it, but I'm serious about this."

"My dear Chester, I'd love to see you in London, of course, but absolutely and entirely without any idea of matrimony, please. You must suit yourself about that."

He left me at Alix's, and walked back to his hotel. I felt faintly annoyed with him, but I liked him none the less. He had slipped into what I suppose he would have called a proposal, casually and lightly, as though it were all in a day's work. He had slipped into it at the end of a story about another woman, another love. I had expected better of him. Therein lay my disappointment. He was, in other ways, intelligent and companionable, but his entire ignorance of women shocked me. And he was proud of this ignorance. He seemed to think it desirable to be ignorant. Why? Why should men—or Anglo-Saxons, and especially Americans—think it desirable to know nothing of women's feelings? Richard, because he had intuition and faultless taste in those matters as in others, was incapable of making a mistake, but I looked on him as a rare exception. Only jealousy occasionally made him stumble. Roland had a vision for ever before his eyes of a woman in a ball-dress and long gloves; a woman without a body—a lady. I had tried to shatter it, but in vain. There it remained until the end. He never forgave himself for the night I spent with him, when the ball-dress and the long gloves vanished—but in his imagination I resumed them again at marriage, for ever. Dear Roland, best of men, and least imaginative; he endured his sufferings with a dreadful fortitude that nearly broke my heart. I could have borne it so much better if he had protested and rebelled, as Alan would have done, as I myself would have done. It was the fortune of war—and he was luckier than some—plenty of boys had been killed or made cripples at eighteen, without having lived, and he was a man of forty-two, who had loved and been loved. It was in that spirit that he died—almost happily. England had done her part, and more than her part, in the greatest of all wars. He, too, had done his part. It was rough luck on me, he said, to be married to a cripple, but it would not be for long. He often talked about those two weeks at Grasmere. All the romance of his life was packed into those two short weeks. I have built a monument in my heart to that amazing and wonderful simplicity of his, and not a day passes without a little tribute being laid there. "Here lies the best and least complicated of men——"

Chester kept away from me for forty-eight hours, and then turned up again as though nothing had happened. But he had been thinking a good deal.

Alix, in her cool way, liked him very much and

199

hoped I would marry him, but I assured her there was not the slightest possibility of it. We were serious people, at her house. The talk was serious, but I liked it. It was shop, but it was most interesting shop.

I began, while I was there, to take fresh stock of my life, looking it over as a farmer looks over his crops and acres. I was now very much my own mistress. The income I derived from books was increasing surprisingly, and with the addition of Roland's pension, I had enough for my mother and myself. She had spent the winter with me, but at present she had a cottage at Bournemouth, where Celia Lawton was staying with her, and she was quite content. I had a comfortable studio flat in London, where I could entertain a little, and where I could both write and paint at my ease. Life was sufficiently interesting, and I had more friends than I had ever dreamed of possessing. I made country-house visits, met people who "did things," and now and then made short trips abroad. All this was very satisfactory, and yet I was aware of one tremendous lack. There was no one in my life with whom I could really be myself, with whom I could share every feeling and express every thought, creditable or discreditable, and that was a very real lack indeed. I now had more confidence in women; I knew they were not my enemies, and they interested me profoundly, both by their likeness and their unlikeness to myself. Yet I could never get over the habit—it may have been the writer's habit—of watching and studying them, and that, of necessity, interposed a distance between us, of which, perhaps, only I was aware. I knew they did most things far better than I did. They bought dresses and hats with more discretion and certainty. (I had spent so many years without buying these things at all, that, when I could buy them, they presented all sorts of problems to me.) They knew all about servants, secretaries, nursery governesses, and the way to write to a Bishop. They were far better at small talk, and could discuss a book without troubling to read it. They knew exactly where to go for a certain kind of silk stocking, and how much to pay for it, and by the time I, too, made this discovery, they had gone somewhere else. They knew amusing gossip—I never knew any, and if I were told, could not remember it—and they related it divertingly. They were charming to me, and never seemed aware of the vast gulf I imagined lay between us. But I never felt I was getting anything from them but copy, and a pleasant kind of affection, and they made great demands on my time, and were frequently annoyed with me for not going to tea with them, or for refusing to play bridge in the afternoons. And yet I liked them, was fond of them, and was grateful to them for liking me.

Men, as I told Chester, I could not do without. And that was chiefly because they both would and could talk. How often I have tried to talk to women about the things I felt, and imagined they must feel, too, only to see in their eyes a little restless, vague look, a little, wandering look—and to hear them say, "Tell me what you did last week—have you been to any theatres? What did you think of So and So?" Alix, of course, would talk about re-incarnation, or psychometry, or Atlantis, or ectoplasm by the hour, but I have met few women who would risk comments on that tragi-comedy, life, or commit themselves in any way to definite views concerning it, or concerning death, or God, or genius, or poetry. There has never been a woman philosopher. I wonder if there ever will be? There may be great women specialists; I doubt if women will ever be unifiers of knowledge.

Chester got very little comfort from Pierre Morin.

"You want a mystic," he told him. "I am only a scientist."

Chester longed to be told that the evidence for some sort of life after death was overwhelming. But Pierre Morin, like Richet, remained a sceptic; while admitting the existence of so far inexplicable phenomena, he refused to grant to them any unearthly significance. The capacities and functions of the human mind itself were as yet too uncharted.

In the Morins' house was a long drawing-room,

running the whole length of it, and partly divided by glass doors, over which a curtain was sometimes drawn. I had been out with Chester one afternoon, and he had left me at the house at about six. I opened the front door with a key Alix had given me, and went into the drawing-room to look for her. She and Pierre had been at a "sitting" the night before, which had kept them up very late—I was not present —and I found Alix with a book in her hands asleep in a deep armchair by the fire. I did not wake her, but went through the glass doors to the other end of the drawing-room and lay down on the sofa there to read through the manuscript of Chester's new book, which he had just given me. It was the biography of a certain aristocrat whose head fell under the knife during the Revolution, an abrupt and unfortunate termination to a life that promised to be a brilliant one. Hundreds of letters written by this man to his family had come into Chester's hands, and he had spent two years translating them and gathering up the threads of his hero's life.

Absorbed in this, I suddenly heard voices in the next room. It was the voice of Pierre that I heard first. He had come upon Alix asleep, and was gently waking her.

"Chérie! Chérie! Ouvre tes yeux!"

There was something in his voice that I had never heard before. I heard Alix murmur, "Pierre," in a drowsy voice, unlike her usual one. So they had their moments, these two! I thanked heaven for it, and wondered, uncomfortably, what I should do. It was a moment I did not wish to interrupt—I felt it was better to eavesdrop than to interrupt—so I made no sign. He began to talk to Alix in French, in a low, pleading, passionate voice. He spoke of his long waiting for any sign of response or change of heart, in her. It was a voice to charm a bird into a net. It was the voice of a lover, a patient, watchful, unselfish lover, who had known how to wait, and, in waiting, how to further, by the most delicate diplomacy, his own cause. I had been right. There had been a pact of some sort—— Oh, wise and patient Frenchman, who had understood so well and with such sagacity the strange nature of the woman he had married, at the same time acknowledging and making allowances for his own physical drawbacks, and by the use of a powerful and delightful mind, overcoming both! For he had overcome them. Her little, broken sentences told me that. I pressed my hands over my ears, and prayed that they would not discover me. I waited for some time, trying to hear nothing, then finally I listened again. There was complete silence in the room. I tiptoed to the glass doors and looked. They had gone. I felt that their marriage began from that day, and on the soundest of foundations. I envied them, and yet I would not have changed places with either for anything in the world.

My visit came to an end at the beginning of the next week, and I returned to London, sorry to leave them, sorry to leave Paris, which was assuming a brisk, wintry sparkle, but anxious all the same to get back to my studio, and to a new book I had been planning. Chester had not spoken of his feelings for me again, but I could see that he was biding his time, and hoping for further opportunities in London.

My studio flat was in Westminster, in a little street not more than ten minutes' walk from the Houses of Parliament. I had one maid, a pleasant, devoted, quiet woman who had once been a member of the Brotherton household, but had left it because she disliked being with other servants. She suited me, and I suited her. She had been at Grasmere that summer, and often told me how she had seen Roland and myself starting off for walks, and had said to herself, "That'll be a match." She thought very little of men, doubtless for reasons of her own which she did not choose to divulge, and the only visitor of whom she approved was Richard. When Chester Dellamere appeared a day or two after my return, and made himself at home in the studio at tea-time, she was both curious and anxious. She alluded to him as "the American gentleman," and looked upon the flowers he brought with suspicion.

Weakly, as was my habit, I had allowed myself
to grow quite fond of Chester. I liked his sallow
face, his smile, his unassuming manner, his modesty,
both national and personal, and he had not yet begun to bore me. He agreed with Schopenhauer that
"if a man is proud of being a German, a Frenchman
or a Jew, he must have very little else to be proud of."
He was not at all effeminate, neither would I have
called him a very masculine man. He was too happy
to sit and talk, to do nothing in particular, to make
himself useful and pleasant, to be an escort, and he
never seemed afflicted with that masculine restless-
ness that makes so many men difficult companions. I
found myself talking to him as I would talk to another woman, and although this was, perhaps, no
compliment to him, that aspect of it did not, appar-
ently, strike him. I knew that he had lived with his
mother until her death, two years ago (except for
that brief interval which was his married life), and it
explained much.

He had never before spent much time in London,
and now began to love it. He wanted to live in London, but problems of income tax worried him. He
wanted to take a small house in Westminster, and
marry me, and live in it. He would cheerfully pay
income tax in both countries if I would marry him.
He thought he could write better in London, he
thought I could help him and he could help me.

Again and again I told him that it was quite impossible, that I did not love him, that I never could love him. I introduced him to Richard, who liked him—how quickly men differentiate between those men they may be jealous of, and those they are sure they need not be jealous of!—and Chester said in his formal, quaint way, that it was a privilege to know such a man. My women friends, too, liked him enormously. He was precisely what they expected a cultured American to be, and he did not mind tea-parties.

But he kept on wanting to marry me. He pictured a life with me in London that pleased him, and he could not bear to give it up.

"Listen, Marna, I know you don't love me, but you're fond of me, and that's good enough for me, for a start anyhow. Look how the Morin marriage has turned out——"

"My dear Chester, do you think I'm like Alix? Do you think you're like Pierre? Why compare two people with two other people who are entirely different?"

"But you like me to go about with you, you like talking to me—or you seem to—I get on well with your friends—we'd have a mighty good time, if you ask me. Your friend Richard likes me, I know he does."

"Only because he knows perfectly well I'm not thinking of marrying you."

"Well, he'd better not be too sure. You might change your mind."

"There's not a chance of it."

I introduced him to a very charming girl named Rhoda Tarrant, whose father was a wealthy peer with a country place in Hertfordshire. She was a pretty and tolerably intelligent girl, without an atom of self-confidence, and she longed to marry. She was twenty-nine, and complained that all the men of a suitable age for her had been killed in the war, but even if they had not been, her diffidence would have kept them at a distance. She was thoughtful and bookish, and not at all fond of games. She liked Chester in her shy way at once. American men were so easy to get on with, and had so much to say—he was a writer? —she would read his books immediately.

Chester thought her a nice girl, and absolutely without any airs or affectations.

"It hasn't spoilt her, being the daughter of a lord," he remarked.

Much as I liked him, I began to wish he were not so much on my hands, for he never made a move without consulting me, and I wanted to get on with my new book.

Rhoda asked us both to Hertfordshire for a week-end, and we went. Chester was delighted with everything, and had a great success himself. When we got back to London, he seemed more restless and moody than was usual with him. I saw him the next day, and he said he supposed he ought to be thinking of going home, and anyway, he was getting tired of hotel life. Two months of it in Paris—three weeks of it in London—it was more than he liked. He thought he'd better get back to Philadelphia. The proofs of his new book would be ready soon, and it seemed hardly worth while having them sent over. Then he burst out:

"Marna, I can't stand it any longer. Once and for all, why won't you marry me? I'll live how you like and where you like. We get on all right. I'm absolutely crazy about you, and you're fond of me. You've got to marry somebody. You can't go on living like this for ever. You may never meet anybody you like better than me. How do you know you will? Perhaps you'll never marry at all."

What he wanted was a home, someone to look after him. He kept protesting his love, but never once had he given me the impression of a man in love. There was nothing about him of the amorous male; he was merely an irritated author.

"Don't worry about me, Chester. If I don't find a husband, I'll take a lover. Probably it would be safer in the end. And once and for all, I've no intention of marrying you."

He was looking at me curiously, surprised and startled.

209

"Do you mean you're serious about that? That you would actually take a lover? A woman like you?"

"Why not a woman like me? I've been remarkably fastidious and self-denying. I'm not a child. To whom would I be doing harm by taking a lover? Tell me that."

He was shocked and uncomfortable.

"To yourself, I should think."

"How would I be harming myself?"

"Well, I shouldn't have thought you were that kind of woman."

"What kind of woman?"

"Oh, Marna, you know perfectly well what I mean. The sort of woman who would take a lover lightly— a light woman."

I had to laugh.

"But I didn't say I'd take one lightly. And if I did, what of it? How does that make me a light woman? I'd be exactly and precisely the same woman as I am now."

But he belonged to the type of man who considered love, outside marriage, as a privilege of the male.

"When you talk like that, I realize I don't know precisely and exactly what sort of woman you are. I thought I did, but I don't."

"But, my dear Chester, I've often expressed my views on these subjects before."

"Well, yes, but I never applied them to you. Oh, hang it all, I hope I'm broad-minded myself, but I simply can't connect that sort of thing with you, or with any woman I like."

"What a strange creature you are! Supposing I said I'd take you for my lover?"

He got up and paced about my studio, his hands behind his back. He replied with at least commendable honesty,

"Well, I'd jump at it, but I wouldn't look upon you as the same kind of woman I do now. I'd feel absolutely differently about you."

(How like Roland, I thought!)

"And how would you feel about me?"

"I wouldn't have the same respect for you I have now."

"And yet I should be honouring you by the gift of myself, without, at the same time, demanding your life-long support and life-long tolerance. Without, in fact, demanding anything."

"You're making me sound like a prig," he protested, "but I can't help it. That's what I feel about it."

"Then I suppose the less a woman gives and the more she exacts, the more you respect her. That naturally follows."

211

"I don't know that it does. But at any rate, the more a woman demands and expects from a man, the more she's likely to get."

"But look what I'd be expecting from you if I decided to take you for a lover. Look at the confidence I'd be placing in you. It's as though I were to hand over my entire fortune without even asking for an I.O.U."

"Then a woman like you has no business to trust any man to that extent."

"If I were to take a lover, it would be a man I trusted entirely. It would be a man with a sense of proportion and a sense of humour, and the discernment necessary to understand the situation. From the moral standpoint (whatever is meant by that) I think it would be less reprehensible than your own action in marrying a woman, yes, committing solemn matrimony with a woman for whom you had nothing but a violent and ephemeral passion. That was cynical, insincere and altogether unworthy of you."

He sat down, and clasped one knee with his hands.

"Yes—well, I admitted it was pusillanimous, and that I was disgusted with myself. Only I felt I wanted to tell you."

"Naturally. Why shouldn't you have told me? I am only pointing out to you, or trying to—no, it's no use—I see it's no use. The whole position of woman on this planet has got to be revised—is being revised—but the news hasn't reached you yet. Go home, Chester, I think I want to write."

He got up, but hovered.

"Marna, I confess I don't understand you. If you're fond enough of me to be willing to live with me, I don't see why you won't marry me."

I stared at him.

"Did I say I was willing to live with you?"

"Well, I certainly thought you did."

I seized the first book my hand could reach and threw it at him.

"Chester, if you don't get out of this place in ten seconds I'll throw the lamp at you. Go away, and don't come back till I ask you. I've had enough of you for awhile."

He went, and I went to my writing table trembling with a kind of fury. I tried to write, but I was too angry, too annoyed. Then suddenly I saw the humour of the situation and burst out laughing. I made a short entry in my diary.

"December 14th. I sent Chester away, after throwing a book at his head. He is a good soul, and it was entirely my fault, but oh, what wouldn't I give—ten years of my life would be nothing—for a man who would be able to think clearly and honestly, even about sex? And when I told Chester that to him women were either goddesses or dirty jokes, I 'said a mouthful,' and it applies to ninety-nine men out of a hundred."

I did not hear from him, nor did I send for him. Then I had an ecstatic letter from Rhoda Tarrant, written from their house in Cavendish Square.

Darling Marna,

Father and mother had asked some people down to Mittering Place for the week-end, and they had omitted to ask anyone for me, so I suggested your nice American friend, Mr. Dellamere. They had both liked him so much when he was there with you. Luckily he was able to come, and was with us from Friday to Tuesday. He got on so well with everybody, and really enjoyed it, I think, and he came back to London in the car with us on Tuesday afternoon. It was angelic of you to introduce him, there are so few really nice unattached men about, of a suitable age, and he has such a delightful mind. He is giving me the manuscript of his new book to read—it's going to be published quite soon in America. I've just started it. It's about a delightful French writer, who was guillotined, quite young, during the French Revolution. I expect he has told you all about it. Father has taken a great fancy to him—you know he always likes Americans—and he is coming to

dine here on Friday night. Will you come, too?
Do, like a dear. Dinner at half-past eight, as
usual. Professor Spurling is coming, and you
know you always like to talk to him. I'll put him
next to you at dinner.

With best love,

Rhoda.

I rang her up and said I should be delighted to
dine on Friday night. Something was going forward,
I thought, between those two, and I felt I must tread
delicately, as one walks lightly and with care before
an oven door when a cake is baking inside.

Chester was extremely glad to see me on Friday
evening, and a little effusive. During the evening I
watched him. What a curious little personality, I
thought, half man, half ink-pot! Half savant, half
crude undergraduate! I had got fond of him, and
I could not get unfond of him in a hurry; though I
now felt a slight contempt for him, I thought I could
like him all over again once he was married to someone else. He was beautifully polished, beautifully
dressed, his sallow face was excellently well set off
by the black and white of evening dress. He looked
distinguished, and his manners were perfect. To
Rhoda's mother, Lady Severfield, he was like a hum-
ble lover, and in his manner was precisely the right
amount of deference. With Lord Severfield he was

215

understanding about port and politics. With Rhoda
there was something hushed and folded in his look,
something devout. I watched, and was amused, and
was a little ashamed of myself for watching.

A few weeks later Rhoda rang me up and asked
me if she might come to tea. She came, and she was
big with news.

"Marna, you've always been so kind to me—I
don't know why you were, when you're so busy, and
so much in demand, and I'm so shy and stupid. But
I've got to thank you for everything—everything.
Oh, Marna, I'm so happy. Chester and I are going to
marry, and I wanted you to be the very first to know."

I expressed my surprise and delight, the first a
pretence, the second entirely genuine.

"My dear Rhoda, how lovely! It's the first match
I ever made in my life—how lovely—it's the nicest
thing that's ever happened. Are your father and
mother pleased?"

"Yes, awfully. They simply love him. And he
wants to live in England half the year—and I do so
hope he'll consent to live in America the other half,
because I've always longed to live in America. Do you
think I can help him in his writing? I do hope I can.
You know I've always read a lot, and I could help
him with the historical part, and research. Oh,
Marna, I'm the happiest girl, and I don't know how

216

to thank you! Honestly, I don't—I simply must give you a hug!"

She told me all about his charming nature, about his reverence for women—"I don't think Englishmen ever feel that enough"—about his devotion to myself.

"He says that, next to me, he thinks more of you than of any woman in the world. I suppose you know about his early marriage. What a tragedy, wasn't it? I feel I must make up to him for that. It must have been a ghastly thing to happen to so young a man."

They were to be married in a month's time, and then set sail for America. It had long been a dream of Rhoda's to go to America.

"He must know lots of interesting people, the sort I always longed to meet here, and never did—except you. And Marna, I'll tell you a queer thing—he's got exactly the same dread of dying that I have. We've talked and talked about it. Ever since I was a child I've hated the idea—but now we both feel it will be easier to face it. Perhaps it's because we've both been so lonely, and won't be any more."

He came in at six, to receive my congratulations. He was quiet, moved, genuinely happy, and, I think, as much in love as he was capable of being. He had found a goddess—out of Debrett. He had come to Europe asking for an answer to the greatest of all mysteries. His mouth had been closed with a kiss. But for years I know he wondered about me. Was

217

I really a "light woman," or had I been pretending to him that day? And so ended another episode. I had made two people happy—I think they will be happy for quite a long time—and I had added something to my little store of knowledge of mankind.

CHAPTER IX

T is difficult to analyse one's feelings about the post-war world. It is difficult, out of the mass of shifting views and impressions, to select a few here and there that are significant. It is certainly a world where everything matters a little less. We have adopted a habit of looking at ourselves through the small end of the telescope. We have recognized the fact that we are dwelling on a fifth-rate planet, and on a fifth-rate planet almost anything unpleasant may happen. Religion has retired to a distance, a little sulky and hurt at being left out of the children's games and pastimes, and is trying to think out new ways of interesting and attracting them. She broods, disconsolately and apprehensively, as she watches them play with toys for which she has no use and which she does not understand—now they are engaged in bending a ray of light—surely that is not a toy for children—now they are playing that dreadful Space-Time game, in which some of them will undoubtedly be lost or hurt; it is all very dangerous and frightening—why could they not be content with Forfeits? She had looked on and shuddered not very long ago when they were pretending to be monkeys, and were climbing trees and swinging from branch to branch, but that was nothing compared with this. Why could they not all come indoors and sit quietly, while she read them fairy stories out of a nice book?

Before the war, I had seen myself as an insecure and drifting fragment in a large, orderly universe. (Or so it seemed to me.) I now saw myself with fairly definite opinions and tastes, and a tolerably secure place in life, in the midst of an insecure and drifting universe. This complete reversal of things amused me. Part of it was due to the experience of growing up, part of it to the fact that a world-war of the most unpleasant character had cut my life in half, so that I was able to look before and after, and observe the immensity of the change.

As for people, I now liked two kinds. I liked people with brains and tongues, who were not ashamed to use either, people with thoroughly sophisticated minds and tastes; and, on the other hand, I liked people who were merely decorative, amusing and pleasant. And in between these two kinds lay the great, ubiquitous majority, whom one did one's best to avoid. The man I really cannot endure is the man who makes a solemn god of business, and the woman I cannot endure is the woman who thinks it really matters if she does not get asked to the So-and-So's ball, or if someone dances somewhere with too few

clothes on, or if her daughter's bridesmaids wear blue
or pink at the wedding.

I remember, and shall always remember, the London in which I was utterly lost and utterly strange;
where I wandered shabby and alone and poor. I
can recapture thoughts of mine that I thought in certain streets—miserable, hopeless thoughts—"At this
corner, where Duke Street runs into Oxford Street, I
once wondered if I were being punished for something I had *done*, if that was why I was being made so
unhappy. And I remember wondering what it could
have been. Perhaps it was for my shameless behaviour with Frank Bellamy—he might have killed
himself—he nearly did—perhaps it was for allowing
Richard, a married man, to love me. And Alan. But
I was miserable before that. I could not find a sin
important enough, or sufficiently traceable to the evil
within me"; and then something I saw distracted my
attention that day, and I thought of other things.
And there is a certain large and ancient elm tree in
Hyde Park, under which I once sat and thought. "No,
I will never have children. I worry too much. If one
of them were to die it would be like dying ten thousand deaths myself. I could not endure it. Or if
they were very ill—no, I will never have children."
Once I saw a wedding party emerging from the doors
of St. Margaret's, Westminster, and thought, "What
a pity I shall never wear a white satin wedding-dress,

and a veil! It would suit me, but I am not one of those people who will ever wear them." I do not know how I knew that, but I knew, and I never walk past St. Margaret's without meeting the same thought, which seems to linger by the doors.

I was now thirty-eight, and was usually taken, particularly by men, for at least ten years younger. And I felt ten years younger. Impossible that I should already have lived for thirty-eight years! I was getting into middle-age. It seemed absurd. I felt a kind of shame at times, as though I ought to have been able to prevent it, as though I should have done something to avoid it. I was very fluid, I was carried along by time, I did not cling to any one year or group of years, protestingly. I did not look back and say, "That was my best year." I had not had my best year, and I knew it. Some people fasten their hands around the nineties, for instance, and are dragged away, protesting and screaming, as a child is dragged away from a party by a stern nurse. And they never forget it; they keep looking back. That was *the* party of their lives—there will never be such another—and to those people Time is cruel, and takes horrid revenges.

My mother was always happy with the Lawtons. A shy woman, she felt entirely at her ease with them. She did not like being with people who expected her to make an effort. They took her to Cornwall that

222

summer, and I was free to make my own plans. But
what plans? I made up my mind to visit no one.
I did not want to visit. I wanted to be free to write.
I was taking a leaf out of Chester Dellamere's book,
and had chosen a heroine from real life. She was a
Regency lady, with morals as free and loose and generous as her gowns. It gave me a kind of pleasure
to write about her, and I enjoy putting myself in
her place. What fun, if one were not fastidious, to
be like her! True, she died rather miserably, but I
doubt if she regretted anything. And I do not suppose the nature of one's death ever gives great satisfaction. I had a good deal of reading to do, and I
felt that a quiet holiday by myself would be desirable. An elderly, rich and somewhat sentimental admirer with a large house in Hampstead and grown-up
sons had something to do with my desire to leave
England for a while. He was aggressively hospita-
ble, and I was getting tired of his hot-house peaches
and his adroit way of appearing at places where I,
too, was going. His sons were disappointing young
men, and I think he felt that a Woman's Influence in
the Home—— I sent him a discouraging letter and
departed for Paris the next day, and, from Paris,
went to a small summer resort in Normandy, once
recommended to me by Alix.

It is curious to me how few people appreciate
the joys of being alone—for a while. It was three

weeks before I spoke to anyone but the chambermaid, the manager of the small, clean hotel, and a few active, and brightly if scantily dressed children on the beach. And I was perfectly happy. I wrote for three hours a day, swam whenever the tide was not too retiring, and the rest of the time lay on the beach, either reading or sleeping. The food was excellent, the nights cool, the days for the most part sunny. And then there appeared at the hotel the type of man to whom a woman, alone, is an enigma and a challenge.

I am reserved and reticent, except when I am with people I know well, and I have at all times an enigmatic face. I think it is a face that refuses to give its wearer away, for which I am grateful to it. When people have known me for some time they tell me my face completely baffled them at first, for they could not in the least tell what was going on behind it, but that now they see how well it expresses my character. That may be so, I do not know. But for Latins an enigma is nearly always challenging, and the Frenchman who presently arrived and occupied a table near me was obviously determined to clear up the mystery as soon as possible.

He had come to be with a married sister whose villa, overflowing with children and nurses, was only five minutes' walk from the hotel. He was too adroit to attempt an acquaintanceship at once, and bided his time. But it was impossible to avoid saying "Good-morning" and "Good-evening," and after a few days he brought a small and attractive niece to lunch, who, as a conversational gambit, fulfilled every requirement.

Charles Vadier has now become all Frenchmen to me, he was so exquisitely French. It is a great satisfaction to meet an individual of another country who so easily epitomizes in his own person all that one feels about that country. Charles helped me to understand France as no one else could have done. He confirmed everything I had already begun to feel about it, and put me on the track of a great deal more.

He was gay, ready to be amused, and ready to enjoy everything that was superficial, charming, absurd, poetic, and divertingly human. For him there was no such thing as nobility, no such thing as altruism. The weaknesses of humanity delighted him. He saw grandeur in nothing. He took off a reluctant hat to bravery, but to nothing else. He seemed to like children, and was a child with them, without self-consciousness. He had been to school in England, and spoke English fluently with a slight American intonation, for in Paris he knew many Americans. He was Anglo-Saxon in appearance, with a fair skin and light brown hair. His sister, on the contrary, was swarthy and Latin. She had four chil-

dren and was expecting a fifth, and so she did not
wish to exert herself much. Charles sought my society pretty constantly. He said he was under a
cloud, as he had lately contrived to extricate himself
from an engagement with a young, pretty and well-
to-do girl of good family. He had allowed his
mother and the young woman's mother to make the
arrangements because he said that whatever his
mother wished usually came to pass, and that once
the affair was under way, he felt it was as unescap-
able as death. Also the truth was that he found the
girl, whom he had met two or three times, very attractive, and had imagined that she was intelligent.
Then they became engaged—and he discovered his
mistake.

"If you could have heard the inanities and the
clichés," he said, "that issued from those charming
lips! Believe me, I know very well that a man lives
with a woman's mind as well as with her body. Also
she was intolerably vain. After two months of
studied neglect on my part, she broke the engagement.
I was a happy man."

Like Edouard, he was an incessant talker. I suppose there are silent Frenchmen—I have never met
one. And he talked amusingly enough. He had
often heard my books spoken of, and had seen them
in windows of book-shops, and he was delighted to
discover that I was a writer. He had never known

a woman-writer before, he said, with the exception of
a poetess with a heavy moustache.

I admired his active, well-built and muscular body.
He admired it himself, and knew that it stood the
ordeal of a bathing-costume well. He was extremely
naïve and wholly natural, a pagan and hedonist, like
Edouard. He had read a great deal, but along the
most curious lines. He read everything he could lay
his hands on about the Jews (who were going to
possess the world some day, he said), about elephants,
about black magic, about the Byzantine Emperors,
about Napoleon, and about the art of El Greco. He
also knew a good deal about farming and agriculture
—unlike most Frenchmen—and had a considerable
knowledge of astronomy. But he knew most of all
about women. He had had many mistresses, and
some of them, I am sure, were charming. He was as
knowledgable about the female sex as Chester Dellamere was ignorant.

It was his habit to assure me that I was slightly different from every woman he had ever known.

"You are more frank, more honest," he would say.
"You have the candour that one finds usually only in
ugly women, who hope in that way to attract attention.
As a rule, only ugly women tell the truth. You are
both candid and agreeable to look upon. I talk to
you as I would talk to a man; yet I feel toward you as

one can only feel toward a very feminine and attractive woman."

I laughed and let him talk. It was all amusing and unimportant. He understood the game so well, I had no fears for him. He would take whatever he could get; even if he met with total defeat, he would manage to persuade himself that he had had a charming victory.

There was something of the *trouvère* about him. He liked hair-splitting arguments and discussions, usually about love, and he would make his exact meaning exquisitely clear, and with a happy use of metaphor. Clearly he could only be himself with women. And he led up to the inevitable attack with perfect skill. First the mind; first the establishing of confidence; the pretty play of wits. It was as if he said, "You see I am a man who has thought and felt and experienced. Nothing that you say, or are, or do, will be thrown away. You take no risks. You will never be better, more finely understood, or with a deeper sympathy. All the shades of mood and feeling of which a woman in love is capable will be observed, appreciated and made tender allowances for by me. Trust yourself to me, therefore, with perfect confidence."

He now knew I had been a widow for over four years. It was useless for me to tell him I had not had lovers meanwhile, for he simply could not credit

it. No, that was something about which even the most
candid woman might see fit to tell untruths. Also it
was no business of his. But he had his own opinions.
Once married—and living for four years a celi-
bate——?

"Ah, Princesse, Princesse!" he would protest,
laughing.

Then came the light touch of the hand, the accidental contact, the lingering look.

"I am too old a bird to be caught like this," I told
him, smiling. "You like candour; very well then,
I am not at all in love with you. Not at all, not at all.
I am amused by these antics—I can anticipate each
move in the game—and I warn you it is a game without any prizes."

I do not know if it is a habit shared by all Frenchmen, but Charles Vadier had a passion for baths,
and in addition to his sea-baths, would take two and
sometimes three of the indoor variety every day. He
would sing as he passed my door, and sometimes I
would meet him in the corridor wearing a long bath-
robe and over his head a coarse net, to keep his smooth
brown hair in place, for, like the hair of most Frenchmen, it had a tendency to stand up *en brosse*. These
encounters were precisely the same to him as any
other encounters, and he would stop and chat as
though he were in ordinary attire. He amused me,
I liked him, but I could not take him seriously. And

229

yet physically I found him extremely attractive. I could not help imagining him as a lover, and it was easy to guess that he would make a delightful one. Then why not, why not? I wondered. Had I not been cheated of mine, was I to live for ever like a nun, because there was no man I wanted for a husband? And who could be more suitable than Charles Vadier, to whom I would find it so easy to say good-bye whenever I wished? As for him, he was in love, in his own way. All his thoughts and energies were now bent in one direction.

I had to haul out into the light of day all my feelings and prejudices concerning love and lovers. I asked myself why I hesitated? Was it on moral grounds? No. Surely a woman of my age need not concern herself with these. Religious? I was not at all religious. I only wished never to hurt anyone and never to lower myself in my own eyes. I had not been inside a church since I was sixteen, and had no desire to go. I had certain ideas about a God, culled from various philosophies; a love of Good and a desire to seek it; and a great love of beauty. I thought there was much confusion of thought everywhere about sex, and that I, too, was confused, though I did not think I was as confused as the Church was, or as the generation before me. I had never found anyone whose views on the subject struck me as clear and sound. It seemed to me that the Greeks came nearest to putting it in its right place, and, having done so, they went on with the business of living with clear eyes and minds. It seemed to me that we, the Western world, needed a new prophet, a combination of Plato and Voltaire—Voltaire to supply the scorn and the humour, Plato the calm analysis and judgment. I could do no harm to Charles Vadier by accepting him as a lover, and I should be in no danger of complicating my own life, for I knew I could never seriously love him. And it was just there that the difficulty lay; it was because of that that I drew back. If I had loved him, I would not have hesitated, and that is exactly the difference between women—or fastidious women—and men. Women are intensely selective; their instinct is to specialize, to concentrate; men's instinct—more often handsomely overcome than women realize—is to diverge, to disperse, to scatter.

And yet he had so much to recommend him, and the only love now in my life was the ascetic yet jealous love of Richard, which remained precisely what it had always been.

Charles Vadier was perfectly aware of the struggle that was going on in my mind, because he had a sort of extra sense about such matters, and could deduce an internal drama quite correctly from the flicker of an eyelid. His voice took on new cadences, his look new meanings. He spoke my name as it had never been spoken before, and I was forced to admire the exquisite pains he took with every little act and word. And he never for an instant gave up the other business of interesting me.

He told me about a certain secret society in Paris whose object was the cult of Evil by the performances of Paphian rites. He had been to one of their meetings, and it had so aroused his laughter that he had had to hurry away.

"They are so solemn," he said, "they are only imbecile children playing with very dirty mud pies."

But he had the inordinate and, I think, intelligent curiosity of most of his countrymen, and wished to know, as far as possible, what was going on in the world. Irony, cynicism and a sense of the ridiculous kept him delicately poised, and even his love was very close to laughter.

We disagreed about a vast number of things, but as neither had the slightest wish to convert the other, it did not matter, and provided plenty of ground for argument.

He believed that the two most creative and progressive influences in the world were the inequality of wealth—the doctrines of socialism and communism seemed to him idiot's prattle—and nationality. To be intensely national seemed to him right, proper and necessary. It was national or racial feelings that inspired art and invention. The Jews created in praise

232

of Judaism, the Frenchman in praise of France. Without this—often subconscious—national or racial competitiveness, art, invention, progress would die. There I profoundly disagreed with him, believing that the artist creates because he must, and that art has little or nothing to do with nationality, though it naturally takes on a certain aspect or flavour from the country in which it is born, or which it adopts.

Wars he believed absolutely unavoidable, though he admitted their futility—from the point of view of actual results—and their wastefulness. About these topics we fought endlessly but good-humouredly, and when he felt he had scored some triumph, it was almost as though he had succeeded in a different battle, and one which was much nearer to his heart.

He was moody, and had fits of bad temper, during which, by mutual consent, we kept out of each other's way, for at those times I found him unbearable. He would go off to walk alone, and return sunny and light-hearted. But I knew that for him the thought of the time we were "wasting" was almost unbearable.

As for me, I found this propinquity, this daily siege, subtle as it was, very wearing, and I wished we had not met, so that I need not have been faced with such a problem. I did not want to take any step I might regret, nor involve myself in anything of which I might afterwards be ashamed. But I do not believe that there is a normal woman living (and let us say

233

a free woman) to whom the love and the desire of an attractive man is not a delight and a temptation. And to avoid these nets it is necessary to take a firm stand early in the proceedings. I should have said to myself:

"This is the sort of man who will probably fall in love with you now that you have been thrown together. He has often been in love before, and will often be in love again, but you can be perfectly certain that, unless you take steps to avoid it, you will have a love affair on your hands before you know it. And the best way to avoid it is not to try to please him. Why should you trouble to let him know what you are like, when, by doing so, you will inevitably bring trouble on yourself?"

But the desire to please is planted very deep in us, the desire to do ourselves justice in the eyes of discriminating persons. One's precious personality must not be hidden, it must be revealed. Why should one let people go from one and say, "I have met So-and-So. I found her a dull, uninteresting woman. She had nothing to say, and was not in the least attractive." It takes a genius not to mind this, and I make no pretence of being a genius. Therefore, I was myself with Charles Vadier; knowing what might follow, I could not resist the impulse to be myself—even though it were only my second-best self; for I was not in love.

Sixteen to Forty

Sometimes as he passed my door I heard him linger. I heard, or believed I heard, a whisper. I kept it locked, and once or twice I thought I heard the handle turn. But if it had been unlocked, I am sure he would not have opened it without my leave. Charles Vadier did not make such mistakes as that. It was my leave he wanted, and to that end he exerted every nerve, every resource. And still I asked myself, "Why not, why not?" and could not find the answer. In a world in which one does not get what one asks for, longs for, is it not wise to take what is offered instead?

Charles had come to be near his sister—who lived at Dijon, and rarely came to Paris—and she bored him by her terrible domesticity. She knitted garments for her children and talked incessantly about servants, and about her husband, a stout, kindly, well-to-do manufacturer of valves. Charles considered she had married very badly, and said she had become a kind of matronly turnip.

"And she was quite a charming girl, and used to read poetry and dream. An unhappy or tragic marriage makes a woman more seductive. A happy one makes her like a creature in a farm-yard. If you were to marry happily, you would never write again. I, who wish you to become a great writer, pray that you never will marry."

"No one is going to listen to your prayers, my friend," I replied, "so I won't worry."

"An artist, a professional woman," he said, "ought not to marry. You would be very foolish. You should be free, you should love where and when you please. You should not have to take care of a man and feed him and make him comfortable."

That night he followed me upstairs and along the passage to my room, where he bade me a whispered good-night. His eyes pleaded as I have never seen eyes plead before. He kissed my hand, the back of it, the palm, the fingers, and fearful that he might be seen there I went abruptly into my room and closed the door. Presently, when I was ready for bed, I put out the light and went to the window, and there, underneath it, alone on the terrace, waited the immobile figure of Charles. I saw his lifted face, white in the moonlight. He waited there, silently, watching my window, hoping for a sign. I dropped the curtain and he was still there. I could smell the smoke of his cigarettes, and hear his slight movements.

.　　　.　　　.　　　.　　　.

The next day two people arrived at the hotel in a motor: a large, fair, well-made woman with handsome features, and a dark saturnine-looking man. They came about five, as I was having a solitary tea on the terrace. Charles was at his sister's, and I was thankful to be alone. He never took those extremely expressive eyes from me, and more and more insistently I asked myself: "Why not, why not?"

The new arrivals came out on the terrace and ordered tea. What a handsome creature, I thought, looking at the woman. She was large and firm and self-confident, and her fair skin was becomingly burnt, and made her hair and eyes seem lighter than they were. She talked to her companion with little sallies and smiles, more for the sake of talking than because she had anything to say, and because there was a spectator present—myself. An attractive woman, I said to myself, and Charles would agree with me. A vital, robust, handsome animal. The man was uninteresting. They presently went upstairs, and I heard their voices coming from a bedroom near mine.

Charles and I were both at our respective tables when the new arrivals came in to dinner. I had not seen him that afternoon, and so had not mentioned their presence, as I might otherwise have done, for it was a small hotel, and newcomers an event.

I saw him start when they appeared, then he bowed, got up, and went towards them, and for some moments remained at their table talking. When he returned I saw a dark flush on his face, and he looked faintly disconcerted and displeased. After dinner he joined me on the terrace for coffee.

"Some acquaintances have arrived from Paris," he said. "I wish they had not."

He told me, in answer to my inquiry, that they were a Monsieur and Madame Something, people well known in Paris.

"She is very handsome," I observed.

"Oh yes, that is true. But I wish they had not come. That woman will watch me all the time."

"Why?" I asked.

He shook his head.

"She is the kind of woman who watches everything and makes up stories that are most amusing when they are least true."

But I knew, by some sort of instinct, that there was more in it than that. I knew that at some time Charles had been her lover, and that she knew he was there. I say I knew—I mean I guessed, and I was certain my guess was right.

Charles was obliged to be polite, and to spend a little time with them, and from looks that Madame flashed at him I was more and more confirmed in my opinion. And after three days, Monsieur bade his wife good-bye, and returned to Paris for a week or ten days. I do not think he could ever at any time have suspected what I suspected. It may have happened before their marriage. That I would never know. Charles was not apt to tell me.

Sixteen to Forty

He was in a most difficult position; that was obvious.

"That woman bores me," he said irritably, on the day of the husband's departure. "If it were not for you I would leave this hotel now that she has come here. She has spoilt everything for me."

I could not help admiring her. She was most cordial to me, though she must have suspected almost as much as I did, and seemed delighted to make my acquaintance, which she very promptly sought. She joined us on the terrace when we drank coffee, she begged us to go to the small Casino with her. She accompanied Charles to his sister's house, she was in no mind to be left alone, and all the time she was endeavouring to charm him back to her. Too late—I knew it was too late. There is nothing so dead as an old love, as anyone knows but the person trying to blow on the embers. But her large, blonde presence changed everything for me. Her pursuit of Charles reduced him in my eyes in the most extraordinary way. She had planted herself there in the hope of recapturing him, and the affair made him, in my eyes, slightly ridiculous. She had only ten days or so in which to do this, and she made the most of every moment. She expanded her fine figure, expanded her fine eyes, laughed with wide-open mouth showing perfect teeth, bathed when he bathed, lay in the sun, exposing clear brown skin, and drawing her wrap

239

about her suddenly in affected modesty. He was bored, he was furious, but what could he do? On my account he did not wish to go, and as long as he was there he was exposed to her batteries. His temper became more and more undependable, and I was more and more amused. Was it possible, could it be possible, I now asked myself, that I had ever contemplated letting this man love me? Incredible, incredible! He was an agreeable man, an amusing companion, but how could I possibly have imagined he could ever be more to me? If he did not belong to that woman with the flashing eyes and the fine bust, he belonged to some other woman exactly like her. He had once loved her—he would love other women like her. But me? Oh, no! Oh, no!

It had been a delightful holiday—and I began to think about going. The blonde woman's voice and presence were everywhere. There was no escaping her. She gave no sign at all of being discouraged, thwarted, but kept her head and her good temper, and smiled on everyone. If she and Charles were together for an instant she devoured him with her eyes. She could hardly keep her hands off him. Charles was in despair. Where was I going? He would go, too. He could not stay in the same hotel with that tigress. He could not stand it. He never saw me alone any more—I was changed—yes, I was entirely different. Why was it? Was I so variable?

What had happened? Why did that woman matter to us? Everything had altered since she came. It was intolerable. He would not say to her what he thought; he did not wish to make a scene, but she had come because he was there—so much he would tell me. It was in execrable taste.

I did not tell him I knew that she had once been his mistress and wished to be again. He knew that I knew. It was, as he had said, in execrable taste. But there it was, and she had succeeded in creating the atmosphere of a French farce all about us. It was not an atmosphere I cared about off the stage, and it was time for me to go. Also I felt ashamed —ashamed of what I had thought and felt there, and I wished to leave it all behind me.

The last two days of my stay were made decidedly gloomy by Charles. A man's past is past, and has no right to intrude itself into the present. Also it distressed him that I should guess he had once loved a woman of that type. The day before I left he persuaded me to walk with him to the village, and at the little flower-market he bought me a great bunch of carnations, and carried them back in his arms along the tree-shaded road. I have never seen a more despondent, helpless and disappointed man. Tears of anger came into his eyes once when he thought I was laughing at him, and I assured him I was only laughing at circumstances and perhaps at myself.

"You nearly loved me for a little while," he said, with a dreadful perspicuity I had learnt to fear. "But you will yet. I will make you. I will come to London."

I did not argue with him. I knew it was unlikely he would come to London. Few Frenchmen did, if it could be avoided, for the franc was falling. I said I would let him know if I came to Paris, and that I would not forget him. The next morning he got up to see me off, and pressed into my hands a fat, white envelope. He looked as though he had not slept at all, and told me he had made up his mind to go away the next day and spend a little time, perhaps, at Deauville. He could not even force a smile, and his dejection was both distressing and flattering.

In the train I opened and read what he had written. It was in the form of a diary and covered many pages. It expressed, very clearly and frankly, what he had felt about me from the first day to the last, and was one of the strangest documents I have ever read. In it I saw myself as he saw me. For once I knew—for I think it was sincere—precisely what one man at least observed in me and thought of me. It was undoubtedly a somewhat bowdlerized edition, for there were many erasures and crossings out, but there was nothing in it that offended—and there was much that made me stop and think, and wonder if it were true. He exhibited a shrewd penetration into character and

242

motive that was almost clairvoyant. And on the day when I first asked myself: "Why not?"—it was after he had made it very plain what were his own feelings for me—he had written:

"Into her eyes has come a new look—a look of speculation. I saw it born. She likes what I am, and she has begun to wonder what I might be under certain circumstances. And that is an adorable moment for me, a moment that I have watched for and longed for. It is a little climax in a play that is made up of many, and which is, of all plays, the one best worth playing."

At the end he had written:

"This diary does not belong to me, and never has belonged to me. It belongs to you. Do with it what you please."

I read it through twice—and tore it up. I felt as though I had got into a row-boat for a little excursion, and had been blown perilously near to the open sea.

CHAPTER X

Y the end of the next year I was beginning to pay super-tax, a questionable joy. I now had no fears for my mother's or for my own financial safety, and was investing as much as I could lay aside from current expenses. It pleased me to live quietly and have few and simple things. Poverty, complete and crushing poverty, had so frightened me that once I had struggled out from under its iron fingers I was not at all disposed to be caught by it again. I now dined out more often than I cared about, paid visits here and there when work allowed, listened to oceans of more or less intelligent talk and made, from time to time, new friends. Richard remained devoted, admiring, seeing no change in me, and wishing to see none. I looked, he assured me, exactly as I had looked that night on the boat in my red velvet dress. He managed to see me, busy though he continually was—committees of every conceivable sort seemed to put out long tentacles in his direction and cunningly entangle him—once or twice a week. He no longer had to explain me (protectively) to his friends; I was quite able now to explain myself. A few people told me, quite frankly, that they thought I was his mistress, but when a woman is as fond of a man as I was of Richard, such mistakes do not hurt, nor are they very damaging. No one would have blamed him, knowing the circumstances of his life. And if they would have blamed me, they were not the sort of people I cared to have for friends. And yet the fact remained that we achieved a very perfect friendship that was nothing more. Richard was Victorian in his morality—or perhaps he was beyond fashions —I think he was. At any rate he preferred to love me in his own way, without asking anything from me, as he could give nothing in return. Such was his point of view, and it simplified things for me. Once about every six weeks he went to see his wife, and returned gloomy and heavy-hearted. He would take her toys—she was fond of coloured wax and coloured pictures such as children like—and I know that every one of those visits was torture to him.

He often talked to me about death. He did not in the least mind dying; he only regretted leaving me and leaving the things that had given him pleasure, such as beautiful scenery, pictures, his lovely silver and tapestries. He believed that death meant extinction, and he wished for extinction. If he could have been offered the choice between everlasting life (life that he could not terminate at will) and everlasting death, he would have chosen death. He had

245

grown much greyer, thinner. In the winter, on stormy days, he still wore the long, purplish, heather-mixture overcoat. He now hated politics, and regretted that he was still obliged to associate himself with them. He wanted to go away and live in some beautiful spot in the country (where I might often visit him) surrounded by the things he loved. He wanted time to read and contemplate. Nature drew him more and more, as it must always draw such men, and he longed for peace, and a green shade.

I now enjoyed a pleasant, modest sort of fame. It was not great enough to inconvenience me, but it gave me a quiet and amused satisfaction. I neither laughed at it nor took it very seriously. I was dissatisfied with everything I had so far written, and sometimes when I listened to music or when I was half asleep I had momentary visions of things really worth writing about and was aware of stores of mental energy and invention within myself that I had not yet tapped.

And most of the time I was intensely and maddeningly lonely. I was exceedingly fond of my mother and she of me, but though she was proud of me and grateful, I think she was happiest when she was with other people. I believe the relations between mother and adult daughter are peculiarly difficult, unless the daughter be the mere shadow of the mother. The difference of sex between mother and

246

son makes the relationship an easier and tenderer one, and, had I had brothers, I am sure my mother would have been a happier woman.

I was something of an enigma to most of the men I knew. They suspected the presence of something ardent in me of which my orderly, outwardly placid existence gave no hint. They assumed a hidden, secret life, and I was more amused than annoyed by these assumptions, for I realized there were good grounds for them. Women, on the other hand, envied me my calm. They were willing—unlike men, who look more below the surface—to believe I led a placid, unstirred existence. How delightful, they sometimes said, to live so pleasantly and uneventfully. How wise I was to avoid involving myself again in the difficulties and complexities of marriage. And how clever of me, they were kind enough to add.

To Richard I sometimes let myself go, and confessed my dissatisfaction. There were times when I could hardly bear to contemplate my life; when to look ahead and see the years about to unroll their meaningless scrolls, without bringing me the one thing I most wanted, drove me almost mad.

But he could not endure the thought that I wanted anything, needed anything more than I already had. The thought that I might yet love someone, might yet marry again, was to him a thing not to be faced. I had only to look about me, he would

247

tell me, to see miserable marriages on every hand.
He knew of only one that was really happy. I knew
more than that, but, even if I had not, it would not
have mattered to me one way or the other. Each
marriage is a separate problem, a little sum that
cannot possibly be added up like any other sum.
The components and, therefore, the answer, are always different. Marriage is nothing but two people
living together, and as long as the people vary, the
results vary. And it was not so much marriage I
wanted as the tremendous and enlightening and ma-
turing experience of living with a man I loved whole-
heartedly and without reservations; a man to whom I
could express myself, and who would modify, re-
form and complete me, and whom I might perhaps
modify and complete. I had for years denied myself what might have been adequate or tolerable in
the hope of finding entire contentment and satisfaction—and time was slipping by so fast!

Meanwhile I was now one of the people with
money and friends whom I had once deeply envied
and almost hated. And I watched the spectacle of the
civilized world trying to regain its pre-war equilib-
rium, and to a certain extent succeeding, with fascinated interest. What irritated and distressed me
most of all was the surprising return of the pre-war
mentality. People began to think and feel as they
had thought and felt before, and that was to me a

very disturbing and shocking thing. If *that* did not teach them to think differently, what would? The more irresponsible and jingoistic newspapers in various countries began blithely to talk about "the next war." The old racial antagonisms were still there. England and America continued to administer to each other the old, well-known slaps and pinches. Italy talked bombastically about a Second Roman Empire. France continued to consider herself cruelly and wilfully misunderstood by every country in the universe. There seemed little new abroad but what was merely destructive, and the more ignorant and superstitious talked about the end of the world, and the Second Coming. All the greeds and selfishnesses that the war had temporarily suppressed were once more to the fore. Not to learn from the war but to forget it was the creed of the great majority.

"War makes us look into our hearts," an old man once said to me, "and what we see there makes us resolve never to look again."

In the autumn I went with a great friend to Rome, in her car. It was my first visit to Italy and it enchanted me. We came back by way of Florence, and Milan and the Petit St. Bernard Pass. Arriving in Paris, I remembered my promise to Charles Vadier, and sent him a note, and he hastened to our hotel, with a bouquet. He made a gallant effort to reestablish our friendship on its old terms—or rather

249

to establish it on what he considered better terms. I was a little afraid of the curious physical attraction he had for me, and only saw him when my friend Catherine Sturton was with me. She was a delightful woman of about sixty-five, pretty, a little vain— but vain of her white hair and her presence and her well-carried years—and thoroughly human. She was exceedingly good to me and to all her women friends, but it amused me to see how men still kept their importance for her. She found Charles, she said, adorable. He made himself so pleasant that she invited him to London, to visit her as long as he pleased. He was charmed at this, and his eyes shone meaningly at me. Here he quite understood that I did not wish to leave my friend, but in London, surely there would be opportunities—I lived alone—she assured him he should come and go as he pleased.

"What a dear!" she exclaimed. "And it's plain he adores you. Why don't you think about marrying him?"

I assured her that Charles' intentions were strictly dishonourable; that he was the perfect romantic-amorist, and that nothing was further from his thoughts than matrimony.

"Otherwise," I said, "I wouldn't bother with him, for as a husband Charles would be impossible. As a friend who would like to become something more, I admit I find him attractive."

"Well," she returned, "I hope he doesn't think I'm going to further that sort of suit, because I'm not. I've seen a good many liaisons, and I think they're less likely to turn out well, on the whole, than marriages. Besides, you're too frank, too open. You'd hate the deceit."

"Nonsense," I said, "I'm as full of deceit as I can be, and don't you forget it. I've deceived all but a very few people all my life. Most of my friends think I'm cold, placid, self-sufficient, simply because I listen to them instead of talking about myself. You know me better than most women do, but even you don't know how lonely I am, how I hate this sexless life, how angry I get with myself because I don't seem able to take lovers light-heartedly, or a husband prudently. How bored I am with my own fastidiousness, which I suppose most people would call virtue."

"I'm not quite such a fool as you seem to think," remarked Mrs. Sturton. "I've guessed all that ever since I first knew you. I don't really want you to marry Charles Vadier. He's too superficial. I only suggested it because I wanted to find out what you thought of him. I'll tell him I can't have him in London after all. It would only be awkward for you."

"Oh, no, not at all," I assured her. "Let him come. I needn't see him unless I please."

We returned to London the next day, and I was soon at work again, feeling rested and refreshed. I had thought of a new plot quite suddenly while we were motoring through the Apennines and I wanted to make a rough outline of it while it was fresh in my mind. My mother came to spend the winter months with me, as her custom was, and I bought her a small car and hired a pleasant young chauffeur, who liked taking such an enthusiast about. She liked to sit in the front seat and he even taught her to drive, although she only took the wheel in the country, and then without a great deal of confidence.

Richard suddenly bought a small house in Brook Street, and filled it with his lovely furniture and stuffs. He had felt for a long time that he was too much with his brother and sister-in-law, and he was tired of the service flat in Bury Street that had long been his only London home. He had a dear old friend named General Blancheard, a stout, jolly, lovable soul, whose little eccentricities pleased and amused Richard. He had a passion for shrimp paste and rum punch, and both of these things Richard always thoughtfully supplied. His affection for Richard was immeasurable. I know he would have undertaken anything for him; he would have died for him. Knowing his idol's fondness for me, he took me also to his heart, and the three of us often dined together and sometimes went to the play. Richard

252

never had a pain or an illness without the General rushing to see me, or ringing me up to find out if I thought it serious. He liked talking about him, telling me stories of his youth, and this never bored me. "In the event of his death," the General once said to me with grave face, "we must collaborate to write his memoirs."

He took it for granted that I would have married Richard had he been free, and I let him think so, because I had almost come to believe it myself. What better thing could I do, from any point of view? It would give him great happiness. It was true that I wanted something very different; I wanted to marry someone younger, more like myself, more vital, someone whose life was still before him, as I felt, at moments of insight, that my own was before me. But what grounds had I for believing that such a man would ever come my way?

Richard asked me to go with him one evening to hear a symphony concert. Orchestral music was the only kind he really cared for, and this was to be an evening of Beethoven. I put on a new dress that night, a green and gold brocade over which he went into ecstasies.

"What wonderful stuff! What a lovely colour! Oh, how delightful! I've never seen you look better. You're in great good looks to-night, my dear. I'm proud to be with you, as I always am. You cannot call your Richard unappreciative, can you?"

The "mode" meant nothing to him. He was barely aware of it, and if it did obtrude itself upon his notice he was apt to think it hideous. He liked women to be feminine, to wear beautiful stuffs and colours. He liked to touch a lovely silk or brocade or velvet. Women's hair, too, appealed directly to his senses. He liked to see ropes of it, coils of it. That I had never cut mine was due partly to this feeling of his. His tastes were pure Gothic.

The music, and his delight in my appearance, moved him that evening. He looked at me with a kind of brooding tenderness. He was sad and yet happy. It was a mellow sort of sadness that gave him pleasure, a sadness that he liked to taste.

It was not until toward the end of the interval that I noticed a man in the row in front, and to my left. I thought his head a fine one, and his profile distinctive and unusual. The back of his neck was peculiarly straight and strong-looking, and his head was set on it in a way that pleased the eye. I found myself looking at him again and again, even after the music had started once more. At one time his hair must have been brown, but it was now streaked in a freakish and charming way with grey. It made his face look younger and fresher, and heightened the colour of the skin. It was at one and the same time, I thought, a thoroughly mature face, and yet an untired

one. It was full of a kind of alert, watchful vitality.
I could see that his pleasure in the music was more
cerebral than sensual. His head was slightly bent,
but a pair of very wide-open eyes, whose colour I
could not determine at that distance, watched every
movement of the conductor. I looked at the women
on either side of him. There was a stout, over-
dressed woman on his right, whose high jewelled
bosom rose and fell with—I thought—simulated and
quite unnecessary emotion. I felt sure he was not
with her. On his left sat a middle-aged woman whose
face was familiar to me. For a moment I could not
place her, then I remembered. She was a friend of
Catherine Sturton's, a Mrs. Duff, whom I had once
met at lunch and liked. She turned her head and
whispered something to him, and he nodded. I studied his profile with an odd satisfaction. Why should
I be pleased that his forehead was well formed, with
frontal bones swelling a little above the eye-brows?
Why should I be pleased that the nose was slightly
aquiline, and sprang from the base with a certain
boldness and decision, and was admirably balanced
by a full and rounded chin? Suddenly, as though
in some occult way he had been disturbed by my attention, he turned and looked full at me. Those
wide-open, clear, perceptive eyes looked into mine.
I felt my pulse quicken. I had not been so attracted
by the mere external appearance of a man for years

255

and years—if ever. And I knew the moment I looked into his face that I should be attracted by more than his appearance. When he turned his head away again I made myself think about the music, aware that for ten minutes or so I had not been listening. Music is a great mystery to me, and I am afraid it always will be. I love it, but I love it with a sort of resentfulness, because I understand it so little. I am perfectly aware that I do not listen to it intelligently, that I do not know how. It pleases me with its cadences, its rhythm, its volume, its power to evoke pictures and ideas, but beyond that I do not go. I cannot tell, above a certain level of competence, how well a thing is played. I cannot say that this renowned conductor conducts a certain symphony better than that renowned conductor, though most of my friends seem able to do so. The effect on me is the same, or, if it is not, the difference is due to my own mood. I hate falseness and sentimentality in music as I do in art, but with art I am "inside." I know how it feels to paint a picture; I can see as an artist sees, feel as an artist feels. But music is entirely beyond me, and I love it and am baffled by it.

"I should like to talk to that man about it," I thought. "Richard is exact and precise about some things, but he is not good at describing mental states. He is taking music like a drug to-night."

He had my hand now, and was holding it in his,

between us. I looked at his tired, wistful, beloved ageing face. I loved it, loved it dearly, but it was not an entire love.

The concert over, I felt a powerful desire to go out as close as possible behind the man with Mrs. Duff. I wanted to speak to her. Luck was with me, and I found myself just at her elbow. I could only see the back of his neck, but, as I looked, something stirred in me again. I caught Mrs. Duff's eye.

"How are you? I remember lunching with you at Mrs. Sturton's once. We talked till four. Do you remember?"

"Of course I do. You've been abroad with her, haven't you? She sent me a line from Rome. I haven't seen her since she got back."

"Come and see me one day," I said. "Perhaps you'll come with Catherine. Do. I'd like so much to see you again."

Then I dropped behind with Richard, and we lost sight of them both. I was glad I had known his companion, and that I had spoken to her. It established a connection, and I very definitely wished to establish one.

"Who was that?" Richard asked. I told him and he said, "She had very nice hair."

We went to supper at his house. General Blancheard was already there, having dined out with friends, and was benevolent and ready to cherish us both.

"I ask you," Richard said, as we sat down at a small table by the fire in his library—there was, among other things, a pot of shrimp paste upon it— "have you *ever* seen Marna in better looks than she is in to-night? Did you ever see a more beautiful dress?"

The General turned his kindly, prominent eyes on me and said his say, with enthusiasm.

"If Leonardo were alive, my dear," Richard said, "he should paint you. I would entrust you to no one else."

"Or perhaps Bronzino," suggested the General, who followed Richard humbly in all things.

I asked, going off at a tangent:

"If any of the great men of the past could be re-called at will, by you, or me, or anyone, I wonder who would be the most in demand?"

Richard said: "Including the great prophets?"

"No, excluding them."

Various names were put forward. Richard said he could only answer for himself, and personally he would call upon Plato, Shakespeare, Goethe and Leonardo, in the order named.

"I would call upon Plato, too," I said, "or perhaps Socrates, or both. Being an author myself, I don't particularly want to meet authors, and I'd only make an exception of Shakespeare, to clear up the tremendous mysteries about him. And I'd like to talk to the shepherd, Cædmon, and find out about those voices he heard. I'd love some homely chats with Abraham Lincoln. Philosophers and scientists would be the most in demand, as far as I'm concerned, but what a bore for them, poor dears!"

The General agreed with me about Lincoln, and said he would also like to talk to Wellington. He thought he might quarrel too much with Napoleon. We all three decided that Lincoln would get a lot of calls from the English-speaking world.

"I'd leave Joan of Arc strictly alone," I said. "I prefer her as a mystery. But there's an author that I really would like to talk to, and that's a lately dead one, Samuel Butler. I'd like to tell him how fond I am of him. He hadn't nearly enough friends here."

We all agreed, and drank his health.

At about twelve Richard took me home. As he left me in the hall of my studio flat he took me in his arms and kissed my cheeks.

"Good-night, dear, bless you! I can never, never tell you what a joy and comfort you are to me. To lose you would be my hell."

I returned his kiss, with affection. To lose him would be my hell, too, and yet I was neither happy nor satisfied with things as they were. I had had an altogether charming evening. To be with Richard gave me an epicurean pleasure. He himself and everything about him had a delightful and rare *quality* that I appreciated and loved. But I longed for something vital, strident, sharp, imperative in my life. Everything seemed keyed down, subdued. He surrounded me with loving-kindness. He was a friend such as few women have. But I wanted to see the lightnings flash in my too low, too brooding sky, and hear the roll of thunder. I went to my bedroom, and suddenly, before I switched on the light, there was projected upon the screen of my mind the profile of the man I had seen at the concert. The conviction began to grow upon me that that man ought to mean something in my life—that he ought to have been in it a long time ago—that he was overdue. Those clear, perceptive eyes sought my own long after I had closed them.

Catherine Sturton brought Mrs. Duff to tea one afternoon. I liked Mrs. Duff. She was one of those much-travelled English women who become ever more cosmopolitan than travelled Americans. She knew Rome, Vienna, Paris, New York, as well as she knew London. Her husband had drunk himself out of the diplomatic service into bridge and inebriety in London, and she could do nothing with him. She had had great good looks which were now waning, but her face was attractive to me; more because of its lines and hollows than in spite of them.

She did not mention the man she had been with that evening, so I, because of my great interest, boldly asked her who he was.

"Oh, that was a man named Channing, Philip Lyall Channing. He used to be —————'s secretary" —(she mentioned the name of a well-known Liberal Statesman)—"but now he writes—chiefly books on industry and economics. That sounds dry, but he's really anything but that."

How British, I thought, amused, to feel the necessity of apologizing for anyone who does anything serious. Imagine, conversely, an English woman saying: "He was a famous Blue at Oxford—tennis and rowing—but he's really quite serious and intelligent." Such things as tennis, rowing, golf, cricket, needed no apology and never got them, but a man who wrote serious books might, unless his friends guarded against it, be thought a prig. Still, I believed Mrs. Duff to be anything but a stupid woman.

She was tall and well-made, and only her face showed the marks of years and unhappiness. I could see that she was impulsive and highly strung and I felt sure she was the sort of woman to attract men to her more than women. On the whole, I liked her even better than I had at first.

Catherine Sturton may have observed my interest that day, or she may not, but at any rate about two weeks later she gave a dinner-party. On the day before, she rang up Mrs. Duff whom she had already invited, and said she found herself a man short. Would she bring her friend Philip Channing? She would. Mrs. Sturton told me she was putting me next to him, and on my other side I would find Charles Vadier, who had arrived that day from Paris.

All the next day I had a curious sensation of things gathering, forming, about me. I had never had it before. It was so strong that on an impulse I rang up a Mrs. Tomlyns, a palmist and a very gifted woman, to whose flat I had once gone with Alix Brotherton. I had sat in the next room while she had her palm read, and when I was face to face with Mrs. Tomlyns, I kept my mouth discreetly shut. She did not suggest reading my palm, nor did I. To-day, however, years after, I felt a sharp wish to see her, and rang her up, without giving my name or Alix's. She very kindly gave me an appointment for five o'clock.

She lived in a small flat in Bloomsbury, and as I climbed the stairs to the top floor I suffered a sharp reaction, and wondered why I had been such a fool as to come. I thought of Mrs. Morisan—of all the silly women I had ever known who went to palmists and seers every few weeks, merely for the pleasure of taking out their egos and undressing them. But when I saw Mrs. Tomlyns again, I recovered some of my confidence. I liked her. She was old and stout and slow-moving, with an expression of great calm and gentleness. I sat down by her and held out my hand.

She touched upon my writing at once. It was an author's hand, she said. I had had quite an astonishing success. She dwelt on my writing at some length. There was another talent—painting—but it had had to be put aside. I would come to it again. What a repressed life mine had been! The early part. How lonely, unsatisfying, cramping. There was always the need of money, often acute. I had suddenly broken away from old conditions—there was an ocean voyage. That was the beginning of it. I seemed to get into other conditions, gradually, not abruptly, and by my own efforts. But helped by a man—and what a man! What a friend! There was love there, physical as well as the other, but it was put aside. There was a barrier between us. He accompanied my life, following it closely, but he was not directly on my line of fate.

"Your marriage," she said (I wore my wedding ring), "hardly counted. It meant very little. It left you almost unchanged. There was suffering connected with it, a great deal of suffering and sadness. He was a good man, but—not for you. But there he is; you had to marry him. You have never met the right man, but you will, you will. You often get depressed, impatient. You almost despair. You were not meant to live alone, you hate it, but have patience. He will come, but you will have to wait. Yes, I'm sorry, but you'll have to wait a long time. There is an exceedingly happy second marriage, but not for a long time." She studied my hand in some perplexity, peering into the palm through a large magnifying glass. "Not," she said sadly, "for perhaps ten years. It is difficult to say exactly, but I think ten years." She studied my face. "You must be nearly thirty," she said.

I laughed.

"Forgive me for laughing, Mrs. Tomlyns, but I can't help it. You depressed me unspeakably for a moment, and now I see you were merely making a slight mistake in your calculations."

"Don't tell me," she said quickly, and peered into my hand again. "I may be mistaken in your face, but not in your hand. No, I can't be making a mistake there. You will marry for the second time when you are about forty—perhaps a little more or a little less." She took my hand in hers and pressed it. "Please, please, I admit I am at sea. I allowed myself to be influenced by your appearance. The lines of your hand suggest that you are nearly forty, your face that you are the same age as my daughter, about twenty-eight."

"I am thirty-nine," I said.

"Then never say so! Never say so! You are not

264

twenty-nine. Not in your body—no, nor in your mind either. It is a young mind. And your body is as supple as a girl's. You can have children, you will have children. You are young. Your point of view is young. You were a long time growing up. And your hands, your body—they are a girl's." She compressed my knuckles, bent my fingers. "A girl's," she repeated. She was genuinely amazed.

She gave me a little sketch of the man I should marry. It was hazy, except that she said: "He looks older than he is—but perhaps it is his grey hair that makes me say that."

I went away feeling that from any point of view I had had my guinea's worth. But that night, when I found myself sitting next to Philip Channing, I began to wish I had not gone. If she were right I had an unfair advantage over him. If she were wrong she was encouraging ideas that had better have been uprooted. However, there we were, and I had never sat next to anyone at dinner who pleased me more.

On my other side sat Charles Vadier, and I know I neglected him, but he had a vivacious and intelligent neighbour in Mrs. Duff, and I did not feel guilty.

Philip Channing spoke quickly and tersely, in abrupt sentences, and often wittily. He had an air of throwing off his ideas hurriedly, because they came so fast. And they were very clearly his ideas, and no one else's. Everything he said was stamped with

his personality. He was nervous; he seemed both
to dislike being there, I thought, and to like it. He
said what he thought, and I never for one second felt
that he was conversation-making. There was a para-
doxical flavour about many of his remarks that told
of an alert and active brain, for when a man says a
thing paradoxically he is seeing two views of it at
once.

He had an entirely personal opinion about everything he touched on, and when he uttered these opinions it was with an air of hoping they would be chal-
lenged which was very stimulating. The expression
of his eyes, which were unusually clear and wide
open, was full of kindness, even sweetness, and this
contrasted in an amusing way with his tart, pointed
utterances. There was a Tory M.P. present whom
he looked upon with some contempt for a speech he
had recently made. I, too, had thought it silly (I
seldom read speeches, but I had happened to read
this one), and we then got on to politics. He said
he was on the side of Labour because it opposed so
much that bored and irritated him. He would have
preferred not to associate himself with any group
or party, but that was difficult to avoid. He disliked
herding. I gathered that there was not very much
about the Labour party—as a party—that he admired, but he thought it vastly less objectionable and
more worthy of support than any other. He liked

men of science and philosophers—any sort of expert, in fact, even golf experts. Charles Vadier told me once he took off his hat to physical courage. Philip Channing took his off to genius.

He had read my last two books and thought them "very good."

"There's no doubt," he said, "that in one thing women are absolutely on a level with men, or even superior to them, and that's in novel-writing. If I were a woman I should certainly want to be a novelist. You are working at something for which you're in every way admirably suited. Women ought to be keen observers—amused, interested and I suppose sympathetic observers. Women, even more than men, as they're less active, ought to analyse and dissect and rearrange. They ought to look on at humanity with a sophisticated smile—a wink in one eye and a tear in the other."

I liked "a wink in one eye and a tear in the other," and thanked him for it. It summed up an attitude of mind I had often striven for. He said:

"I rather think you've got it."

He, like Richard, like all the intelligent men I have ever known, was anti-feminist and pro-feminine. In some ways he reminded me of Alan Morisan; he also was a rebel, but I think a saner, more clear-thinking one than Alan, and less of an extremist. Presently he returned to my writing.

"You have a somewhat satirical pen," he said. "You ought to develop that vein of satire. It's a good one, and too few people have it. There's never been a really good woman satirist. And now is the moment for one."

"What shall I begin on?"

After a moment's thought he said: "Why not the hangers-on of art and music? The people who sit on cushions on the floor, and know all about the painters and writers and musicians that no one else will ever even hear of. The groups there are in every city who talk, talk, talk, and seem to live by taking in each other's toshing. The beautiful young men who sway about the tea-parties with exquisite waists and out-sizes in trousers and half-sizes in brains, saying 'quite too marvellous'; and who flock to the Russian Ballet—I go myself—I like it, but they nearly ruin it for me. W. S. Gilbert satirized them in his own way a little while ago, but it needs doing again, and more thoroughly. The worst bunk of all is talked about art—they have a wider field there and can't be so easily caught out. There's more of this rot talked to-day than ever before in the world's history, I believe, and now's the time to make fun of it. Mencken in America could do it, but he's too busy chastising the Babbitts." He added: "I dare say they're very worthy, nice people, these babblers and appreciators. I suppose we have to have them to counteract the peo-

268

ple who want to know exactly what an artist *means* in his pictures, and think the only type of female beauty worthy the painter's brush or the sculptor's chisel is Gladys Cooper's. Between them they're enough to make any artist who listened to them go and hang himself. But I suppose artists don't listen."

I liked that tart, slightly irritated manner, particularly in so young a man. I judged him to be under forty. And yet he was extremely modest, almost shy, about himself and his own work. He never once allowed the conversation to become personal—or personal to him. On the contrary, he made me talk a good deal about myself—and I was unused to this. It surprised me. But I had expected this man to surprise me.

As we were about to leave the table, he said: "Come and lunch with me one day. Will you? Are you on the telephone? I'll ring you up."

That was all. It was enough. I was satisfied.

Afterwards some of the party played bridge, but Charles Vadier, our hostess, Mrs. Duff, Philip Channing, another man and myself, talked. I was more and more attracted to Philip Channing. I thought Mrs. Duff's manner to him faintly proprietary, and wondered a little. Had she been a widow I should have been a little nervous, but, poor thing, she was not. She was one of those thin, tired-looking women who, I believe, are extremely sensual. She interested

269

me. And Philip Channing and I looked at each other a good deal.

Charles Vadier took me home. Whatever attraction he had once had for me was dead—utterly dead. Being a Frenchman and, therefore, something of an artist in amours, he did not make love to me in the taxi. He was tender, solicitous, and there was that caressing note in his voice that only a Frenchman or an Italian knows how—or is willing—to employ. It had no effect on me whatever except to make me wish to give an imitation of him to Catherine, which would have been unkind; and I told him it was delightful to see him in London, and that I felt sure he would enjoy his visit; and went briskly into my own door, longing to be alone with my thoughts. I was happy and excited. When would he ask me to lunch? How soon? How much had he liked me? How much did he like Mrs. Duff? Not that I cared. If he was for me, he was for me; if he was not—it did not matter.

Our first luncheon was electric, extraordinary. I had never in my life felt so entirely myself, so wholly and exquisitely at my ease. I could feel myself developing like a negative in its chemical bath. It did not matter what we talked about—books, his dislike for priests—I am afraid it was more than dislike—my journey to England before the war, the art school in Paris—(he made me tell him all about this; he loved pictures, but painting was as much a mystery to

270

him as music was to me). While I was with him I
had a sense of being cut off from the world and
wanting to be, that I have never had with anyone else.
If we had been surrounded by people I knew, I
should not have seen them. I had a feeling of lightness, of elation, of all-thereness that I had never
known before.

I insisted on hearing something about his own life.

"Oh, it's very much like anyone else's. I went to
the usual sort of school, then to Oxford, then I was a
free-lance journalist, then my father got me the job
of secretary to a Tory M.P., very much like the one
at Mrs. Sturton's the other night; then I got fed up
with his type of mind and began arguing with him,
and finally threw up the job; then a friend of mine
who had been secretary to ————— suggested that I
take his place, as he was thinking of going into politics himself; I did so, for three years; then he retired,
and I was very glad because I wanted more time to
write; then the war came, and I pretended not to
mind getting into a uniform, which I loathed; then
I went to Mesopotamia, then I was sent home, sick,
then I was sent to France, then demobilized, un-
wounded, God knows how or why, in 1918. Then I
at last got to work with my writing. Three years
ago my father died, and I joined a firm of publishers
—Salter and Marsden—they only publish text-books,
so you probably don't know them. I have a mother

living in Bath, and a married sister in London. I'm
not as fond of games as I used to be, but I'm rather
good at golf in spite of myself. Will that do for the
present?"

"As a skeleton, yes. Your disinclination to talk
about yourself does you credit, but I find it annoy-
ing."

"Do you? Give me time. Eventually you'll probably have to listen to everything I've ever done or
thought. You'll cry for mercy." As he said this he
leaned toward me with a curiously charming and
tender look.

"You darling!" I thought. "You feel about me as
I do about you. You like me, I know it."

"I had a husband in Mesopotamia," I said.

"I wondered. Was his name Roland, and was he
a major?"

"Yes."

"I knew him a little. Not well. Just to say hello
to."

We said no more about Roland just then. I knew
all that would come later. I could see in his eyes,
"A very good soldier, but I wonder why you married him? I shouldn't have thought he was your
type." There was just a shade of wonder, of ques-
tioning, and then we talked of other things.

I found him charming, charming. He had a way
of reducing things to their lowest terms that I liked,

272

of getting at the kernel of things in a few terse words that, as a writer, I envied. And I found a most impish and exquisite sense of humour, quick, unexpected, delightful. I got up from that table as much in love as a woman could be. We walked out of the restaurant into a fog, and he said: "What a nice day!" and meant it. "When will you lunch with me again?" he asked at the door. "To-morrow?"

I laughed and said: "Yes, I will. At the same time and place?"

"Yes, the same place, but a quarter of an hour earlier. Where are you going now? Home? I'll put you into a taxi."

I said I would walk, and we parted. I stopped ostensibly to look in a shop window, but actually to look after him. He had the most engaging back I had ever seen—broad, well-made shoulders, narrow hips, and a youthful, confident walk that I liked. And the back of his neck—I knew what was going to happen to it—and soon—

I was wildly, deeply in love, already, and I wanted to see him as often as possible, wherever possible. I thought I could hardly live until the next day at a quarter to one.

Those greenish-grey eyes haunted me all day. Wide open, candid, intelligent.

"If I had made him myself," I wrote in my diary

273

that night, "I couldn't have made him more to my entire satisfaction."

During the night I woke up and thought: "I *have* made him myself. I've wanted him so long that I've come to believe he exists. But he's really only a creature of my own brain." No, he had sent me a book of his that evening; it was on the table beside my bed, with his name on it. All was well.

That he was immensely interested in me I knew that first day, and the next day it was still more obvious. My curiosity about him was a pale thing compared to his curiosity about me. When did I first begin to write? Why? What was my life like in America? In Paris? What was my mother like? Whom did I look like? Out of the stream of our talk, or the two joined streams, it is difficult to select anything. I only know that my one desire was to make myself known to him, clear to him, to chip away all that was insignificant and concealing, and to come out completely into the light of day.

He thought the sort of life that I had had suited me perfectly.

"It's been complicated and full of contrasts, and that's been good for you. You're complicated yourself, and full of contrasts. I like that."

I did not tell Richard much about him; I wanted to be quite certain, first, that Philip's feelings for me were what mine were for him. Even when I knew, and that was soon enough, I hesitated. To share so prematurely what had just come into my possession, was not altogether to my liking. I did not want to speak of it to anyone. But I told Richard I had met a delightful man, and that I was seeing a good deal of him, but it made no impression on him at the time.

I have never seen a man show what he felt as plainly as Philip did. It shone out of his eyes. He hated to leave me; lingered over our lunches and dinners to the annoyance of waiters, lent me books, and brought fresh ones before I had finished them. Everything he had read and liked I must read. But for days, although he looked at me like a lover every time our eyes met, he said nothing.

Then one night, about three weeks after our first meeting, he came to dine at my flat. I had my meals in the studio by the fire, and when there were visitors I got in an extra maid. My mother was visiting the Lawtons, and I asked Richard and Catherine Sturton to make four. I was anxious that Richard and Philip should like each other, but I knew that it would not affect my actions one atom if they did not. I was beyond being influenced by anything or anyone. I had completely and entirely succumbed. There was not a single dissenting voice. Philip was alert, nervous, watchful, his manner to Richard exactly right. He understood him at once, he knew his type, he knew how to deal with him. And that was not at all difficult that evening, for Richard was at his best and most genial. Philip's awareness of other people's states of mind amazed me. I knew he completely understood Richard's feelings for me, and mine for him. "Let me see how I should feel in his place," he would say to himself, and he would put himself there, and succeed as nearly as possible in looking through another man's eyes.

He looked through mine, too, surprisingly accurately. His active imagination enabled him to shift his point of view with ease. I had not a longing, a wish, that he was unaware of.

After dinner the talk suddenly turned on religion. Here were four fairly intelligent people, none of whom accepted any creed, or church, or recognized the authority of any religious teacher. Richard clung merely to the belief in an unknowable God, a God entirely beyond man's conception. He would have said that religion tried to rationalize something that defies rationalization. God, as taught or described by any of the revealed religions, he utterly discarded. So did we all, except Catherine, who admitted it was because she was too lazy to make the mental effort required even in discarding something.

Philip would have agreed with Spinoza, and did indeed quote him, that: "In so far as the mind sees things in their eternal aspect it participates in eternity." But he was the least ready of any of us to admit to beliefs of any sort. He did not want to cumber his mind with any such undergrowth.

"I'm *afraid* to push my boat into the open sea, as well as too lazy," Catherine admitted. "I tie it up tight to the shore, and hope the rope will hold."

It was a successful evening. They all liked each other. I thought I had never been so happy in my life. The door that had always seemed locked to me was beginning to open.

At half past eleven Catherine said it was time for her to go home, and looked from one to the other of the men for an escort. I said quickly that Richard would take her home, as his car was there, and they lived in the same neighbourhood. So Richard went with her, a little amused, but nothing more, at what he guessed was my intention—to talk a little longer with Philip. He said: "Good-night, my dear, good-night. It's been a charming evening. Dinner, talk, company, hostess, all delightful. I have loved it."

Philip made motions as though he must go, too, but I detained him with a glance. When the door had closed on the others we sat down on either side of the fire. Suddenly he left his chair and came to me and knelt, putting his arms about my waist and his head on my lap.

"Marna, I'm going to marry you, but it will take time. We'll have to wait a little."

I held my breath and said nothing, but put my hands on his head.

He looked up at me.

"You will wait, won't you?"

I nodded, and he clung tightly to me, like a child, his head resting in my lap. I felt absolutely flooded with happiness, too great for speech, too great even for thought, and I leaned my head against the back of my chair and closed my eyes. For a long time we sat that way in silence, while I let my fingers touch his hair and forehead. Suddenly he got up, and lifting me out of the chair, took me in his arms. I put my arms about his neck and we kissed as though we had been in danger of starving for those very kisses.

"Oh, Philip, Philip," I murmured, "I knew, the first time I laid eyes on you."

"You've got nothing on me there, my angel,'" he said, with a flippancy that I soon learnt to expect from him in emotional moments. Then he released me, and went to the fire.

"Oh, Christ! Why have I been such a fool! It'll take time, Marna, and I want to marry you to-morrow, or next week. And I can't."

There were tears in his eyes.

Suddenly I knew. I went to him and put my arm across his back and my head on his shoulder.

"Well, be as *kind* as you can, my darling. And

278

take all the time you want. I'm sorry; for you and for her, too."

Then he told me about it, realizing that I guessed a good deal. He was really very fond of Helena Duff. She was a most unhappy woman, with a husband who was a combination of a bridge-score and a bottle of Scotch. He liked her, very much indeed, and she had borne her troubles almost too admirably.

"In short, I have been her lover for several years," he said. "You must forget it, now that you know it, but I had to tell you. For at least a year I've been wishing that a younger and more ardent lover might come her way; for her sake, as well as mine, but alas, none came. It is almost impossible for a man to extricate himself from such a situation, Marna, without appearing a cad, both to himself and to the lady —the sole objection I have to forming these attachments, which are otherwise very charming." He could talk to me like that because he had complete confidence in my understanding. I said I quite agreed, and he went on: "I was very fond of her, without really loving her. She attracted one or two sides of me, but by no means all. I don't like her any less even now that she knows I want to end it, and is disposed—why, God knows—to want to keep me."

He leaned his hands on the mantel, and his head upon them. "Last week and this there have been scenes such as would draw crowded houses nightly to any West End Theatre."

"You poor creatures!"

He turned a miserable face towards me.

"Oh, Marna, I loathe hurting her, or any woman, but there are moments when I'd give my soul to be a single-minded brute. I want to say: 'Yes, this is all very well, my good woman, but how often have you said to me that a woman who tries to keep a man who wants to leave her, deserves all she gets?' Such remarks used to give me great confidence. And I can't say it, and I can't tell her I never did love her when she talks about 'our wonderful love.' Oh, well! It's entirely my own fault. I know it. If only the position was reversed, how simple it would be! Do you think I'm a dirty dog?"

He took me in his arms again, and I was silent, smiling at him.

"I've got to live with a brain that thinks quickly and clearly, more quickly and clearly than mine does, and you've got it, and I've got to have you. I've got to live with a pair of eyes that looks out and sees the same sort of world that I see, and from the same angle. And you've got them. And what I want and like in the way of a body, Marna, you've been obliging enough to have also. Oh, my darling, I believe you love me! Why do you? What do you see in me? Do you see anything good in me? What is it?"

Sixteen to Forty

When he left me he was confident and much happier. His troubles with Mrs. Duff were by no means over, and he knew it, but he felt better able to face them. I was very sorry for her, but I did not see how I could help her. Philip had never been really in love with her, though he had made her happy; so happy that she could not endure the thought that it was all to end. She could not say—few women can, or men either—"what I have had I have got." She only saw an empty future without him, and I knew what she must be suffering. But if I had sent Philip away it would not have improved the situation in the slightest, and such a proceeding would have been preposterous and silly. What he could not do and must not do was to leave her abruptly. He saw her every few days, and was very tender with her, and tried to make her see that it was now best for both of them to say "finis," and cease to look behind. But it usually ended in a scene, and he would come to me with misery in his eyes, and talk about music, plays, books, persons—about anything but love. And then, when it was time for him to go, he would seize me in his arms violently and wildly, as though he were afraid of losing me, and would then release the flood of pity and irritation and boredom and disgust that was in his mind, telling me the things that had been said, the agony they had both been through.

"These scenes," he said, "absolutely kill all the affection I ever had for her."

One day Catherine Sturton came to me and said that Mrs. Duff had begged her to go with her to the South of France, as she felt she was on the edge of a nervous breakdown. She added:

"I know a good deal about it, my dear, and I think the only thing is to take her away. For all your sakes. And I think that if I were you I would have your plans as far advanced as possible by the time she comes back."

Dear Catherine Sturton—unhappy women found a good friend in her. She said that Charles Vadier had gone back to Paris, very sad at having seen so little of me. She was afraid I had been a little unkind to him.

"I was," I said. "I know it, but I couldn't help it. I couldn't see him, Catherine, I couldn't. I am in no mood now for Charles Vadier."

The day Catherine Sturton and Mrs. Duff left for the South of France was a happy one for my poor Philip. Only I knew, and perhaps Catherine guessed, what a relief it was for him. He was worn out— his emotions had been so played upon that, as a reaction, he had begun to see nothing but the humour of it all. And to a man there is always a kind of grim humour in such a situation. To be wildly and passionately wanted by a woman he does not want is tragic and grim, but sorry though he may be for her, to take it all too seriously seems to admit a consciousness of being worthy of such a love, and a man's sense of humour and proportion rebels. He tries to think, "She is suffering from an unfortunate illusion. She loves something that does not exist. I am quite unworthy of all this. She is making a mistake, and I must try to convince her of it."

There is nothing a woman can save from such a situation but her own dignity, her own pride. She can only say, if she have the strength and the courage to say it, "I love you and will always love you, whatever you may choose to do with your love. But I will not try to keep you, if you wish to go." Then that faintly comic element can never possibly arise.

I was deeply sorry for Mrs. Duff. That she should suffer was natural, and tragic; that she should make scenes was pathetic; but whatever she did, how well I understood her feelings!

I had still to tell Richard.

He was dining with his brother and sister-in-law one evening, and they were then going on to a reception. Richard had refused to go, and came instead to see me. It was about ten. I sat by my fire, trying to find a way of saying what I had to say that would sound least abrupt and crude, when I heard the bell ring. It was a wet night, and he came in with raindrops on his coat; and his face, when he kissed me, felt damp.

He had never held himself very erect, and now his tall figure stooped a little. He suddenly looked ten years older. His face frightened me, when I saw it in the light.

"Richard! You don't look well. Is anything wrong?"

He sat down by the fire, his fine hands held out to the blaze.

"No. I've been worried about this and that! and I seem to have more work to do every year. Next year I really will cut it down, I must. And the year after that I'll stop altogether. I'm getting old. It's right that younger men should take my place. I have never clung to things. I hope I am not greedy. When my time comes, I will gladly step down. I feel nearer to death to-night than I have ever felt before. I don't mind that."

"My dear!" I cried, "what's made you feel it? Why should you feel it? You're not well."

He was silent for a moment.

"I hope I shall know when the moment comes to say good-night. It's a pity we don't know the cue. I should like to be able to say immediately: 'I am ready!' instead of wondering: 'Is this my exit? Is it here I turn and go out?' I have enjoyed my life. Except for one great sorrow, it has been a good life. I have had dear friends; you are the dearest of all. But if the time has come—I am ready to go."

Sixteen to Forty

I slipped from my chair, and dropped to my knees beside him.

"Oh, Richard, darling, don't talk like that to-night. Don't. I was going to tell you a piece of news that I am afraid will make you unhappy, and how can I speak of it if you are so sad already?"

He put his hand on my head. I tried to look into his face, but he averted it.

"I know your news," he said, quietly.

For a moment I could not speak.

"How did you know? Did you guess?"

He shook his head.

"No. No, I didn't guess. I never should have guessed. And even now, unless you tell me it's true, I'll try not to believe it. Catherine Sturton told me just before she went abroad. I met her by accident. She said: 'What do you think of Mama and Philip Channing?' or something of that sort. I said: 'What do *you* think of it?' and I changed the subject. It surprises me a little that I should have heard about it from a third person; that's all."

"Damn the woman!" I exclaimed. "Oh, I'm sure she said it innocently. She thought you knew. But my dear, no one knows. Certainly not Catherine. She only guesses. And that only because there's a woman who was fond of Philip, who suspected the truth, and told her. Oh, my dear, you should never have heard it that way. I'm sorry, I'm sorry. My

285

darling Richard—and for five days you've said nothing to me about it."

"I was waiting," he said.

"It's spoilt everything."

"I don't suppose I should have enjoyed it, in any case," he replied, with a little flash of humour.

I told him everything then. I explained to him that I could not tell anyone at first—I wanted to keep it to myself—entirely to myself. I had told no one but him, no one, not even my mother, who was away and so far knew nothing of it.

We had been through it all before, when I married Roland, but he was still the same, still jealous, sensitive.

"But you like him? You do like Philip Channing? Oh, say you do! You must. You couldn't help liking him."

"I do like him," he said. "No more than that."

"Richard, your fondness for me survived my first marriage. Tell me it will survive this one."

He sighed.

"I feel I am getting too old for these blows of fate. I can't meet them with any elasticity."

"My dearest, you are exactly the same. You are taking this just as you took the other, but better, because you like Philip better."

"I still lose you."

286

"You will never lose me. And I shall be happy, this time. Are you glad?"

"My dear, I have never wanted anything but your happiness. You seem to think you will find it in marriage. I am not so optimistic."

"Only in *this* marriage," I interrupted.

"I pray you are right. You spoke as if I had to be reminded of your right to be happy. Have I ever forgotten it?"

"Oh, my dear, don't misunderstand me. Don't."

He got up soon. His tall figure drooped. His eyes were heavy.

"I must go now. I must think about all this. I wish you had told me sooner."

"I couldn't talk about it. And believe me, I've told no one else. No one. Only you. Kiss me good-night, Richard. I feel miserable. Miserable!"

"Don't, my dear. Why should *you* feel miserable? You have everything before you. I will see you again soon. My love to your mother, when you write. Good-night. Good-night."

And he was gone. I went to bed crying. Could happiness only exist through someone else's sorrow? But I had faith in Philip. He would help me with Richard. He would win him over to a better view of things. He would make me so happy that even Richard would be comforted and reconciled.

He came the next night, and we planned a quiet,

almost a secret, wedding. Richard, my mother, his sister—(perhaps). That was all.

"The less this wedding is like a wedding, the better I shall enjoy it," I said, and he heartily agreed.

I told him about Richard.

"I like him for liking you—for loving you," he cried. "I feel warmly toward every lover you've ever had. Tell me about them, every one of them."

I promised to find a small house within a month. We would hurl some furniture into it and arrange it after we had begun to live in it. We would go abroad for a short trip, perhaps to Rome.

He was wild to begin our life together. I assured him I was scarcely less eager.

"Do you know how old I am? I'll be forty in two months."

"Well, what of it?"

"To think when I was kissing young men at sixteen and seventeen, it was your kisses I wanted. Why have you made me wait so long?"

"Let us piously echo Mr. Browning's remark: 'The best is yet to be.'" He hated Browning for an optimist, and for some other reasons.

He could hardly tear himself away that night.

"My darling, you are the most utterly desirable authoress on Bradley and Stimson's list." (They are my publishers.)

He had a way of laying his head on my breast and

being completely silent that I adored. When I looked down into his face, I would see that his eyes were wide open, and his thoughts miles away.

"I've just thought of something I'd like to say to Dean Inge," he would remark, absurdly.

His thoughts ranged anywhere and everywhere. He thought my brain quick. I thought it ponderous compared with his. I knew that if I lived with him for ever he would never bore me for an instant. He had the adorable trick of unexpectedness. He was quickly touched, quickly moved. In poetry, music, literature, in all things that deeply interested him, his taste was almost infallible. And not the least of the things I loved about him was his ardour. Frankly passionate, frankly delighting in love, and yet in his most passionate moments never far from laughter, he was the lover I had longed for, the companion I had feared I should never find. Sexually I think he was entirely a-moral. He wanted to hurt no one; he would always take care not to cause unhappiness—to him the one great sin—but he was without prejudices. He would protect me from hurt, from himself as from anyone, as he knew I would protect him. When one discovers a treasure one tries to keep it untarnished, unspoilt, if one is not a vandal. The only happiness I now wanted was his, the only happiness he now wanted was mine.

"Oh, if you will only talk to me and love me all

my life," I cried one night, as he was going home, "how happy I shall be!" I kissed the back of his neck, an adorable place.

He took me in his arms.

"Blessed one! Lovely one! Will you always love me? Promise? Because I can never get over you."

And sometimes I would see sudden and unexpected moisture in his eyes.

I stood at my bedroom window the night before our marriage, looking out before getting into bed. I was so happy that I was almost frightened. The night had cleared, and I saw cold stars pulsing and snapping in a frosty sky. I could see over the roof-tops and chimney pots to where, above the heart of London, was the dull red glow of street-signs.

"But why should I be frightened of anything?" I asked myself. "If I should die to-night, what an exquisite ending to my life! If I live, what an exquisite beginning!"

(¹)

THE END

CPSIA information can be obtained at www.ICGtesting.com
Printed in the USA
LVOW080848081211

258416LV00004B/17/P